your RIGHTS at work

3RD EDITION

a *TUC* guide

workSMART
www.worksmart.org.uk

KOGAN
PAGE

First published in 2000
Second edition 2004
Third edition 2008
Reprinted 2008

Apart from any fair dealing for the purposes of research or private study, or criticism or review, as permitted under the Copyright, Designs and Patents Act 1988, this publication may only be reproduced, stored or transmitted, in any form or by any means, with the prior permission in writing of the publishers, or in the case of reprographic reproduction in accordance with the terms and licences issued by the CLA. Enquiries concerning reproduction outside these terms should be sent to the publishers at the undermentioned address:

Kogan Page Limited
120 Pentonville Road
London N1 9JN
www.koganpage.com

© TUC, 2000, 2004, 2008

The right of the TUC to be identified as the author of this work has been asserted by them in accordance with the Copyright, Designs and Patents Act 1988.

British Library Cataloguing in Publication Data

A CIP record for this book is available from the British Library.

ISBN 978 0 7494 5239 1

Typeset by Saxon Graphics Ltd, Derby
Printed and bound in Great Britain by Bell & Bain Ltd, Glasgow

A FIRM COMMITTED TO THE TRADE UNION MOVEMENT

Fighting For Workers' Rights

FIGHTING FOR SOCIAL JUSTICE
• SOUTH AFRICA
• COLOMBIA
• CUBA

www.thompsons.law.co.uk

0808 100 8050

 THOMPSONS
SOLICITORS

THE MOST EXPERIENCED
PERSONAL INJURY FIRM IN THE UK

Thompsons Solicitors is regulated by the Solicitors Regulation Authority

The sharpest minds
need the finest advice

visit www.koganpage.com today

You're reading one of the thousands of books published by Kogan Page, Europe's largest independent business publisher. We publish a range of books and electronic products covering business, management, marketing, logistics, HR, careers and education. Visit our website today and sharpen your mind with some of the world's finest thinking.

KOGAN
PAGE

TUC Best Campaign Winner in 2004, 2005 and 2007

Usdaw – the Campaigning Union

❯ *Visit our website for some great campaign ideas and resources www.usdaw.org.uk/campaigns*

❯ *To join Usdaw visit www.usdaw.org.uk or call 0845 6060640**

Usdaw
Union of Shop, Distributive and Allied Workers

General Secretary: John Hannett
President: Jeff Broome
Usdaw, 188 Wilmslow Road, Manchester M14 6LJ
*Calls charged at local rate

Contents

www.koganpage.com

One website.

A thousand solutions.

You're reading one of the thousands of books published by Kogan Page, Europe's largest independent business publisher. We publish a range of books and electronic products covering business, management, marketing, logistics, HR, careers and education. Visit our website today and sharpen your mind with some of the world's finest thinking.

unionlearn
with the TUC

Changing lives through learning

It's never too late to learn, to develop your skills, and change your life. That's the message of **unionlearn**, the TUC's education and skills organisation, run by the unions for the benefit of members and potential members.

Visit the website now where you can:

- order free materials
- search the publications area and download copies free of charge
- get daily updates of the latest news, details of campaigns, and information from the regions
- join online discussion forums
- find a complete list of all TUC Education courses for reps and officers
- find what you need to know about developing skills for life
- sign up for regular email alerts
- get free expert advice on your learning and career options

www.unionlearn.org.uk

Equal
EUROPEAN UNION
European Social Fund

Foreword

Few people will go through their working life without needing to know something about employment law. That is not to say that most workplaces are full of abuse or exploitation. They're not. Most employers aim to treat their staff fairly, and most succeed most of the time. But even in the best-run organizations, things can go wrong.

Employment rights have become much better in recent years. Unions are often in the news campaigning for new rights and highlighting employer abuse that is perfectly legal. But our desire for a better world should never obscure how much we have achieved since the change of government. Much of this book is taken up with explaining rights that have only come into effect since 1997.

Nor should we leave the European Union out of the equation. Thanks to coordinated union campaigning across Europe we have holiday rights, parental leave and rights for part-timers, and most recently discrimination based on age, sexuality or religion was made illegal. It is unfortunate that little of this is ever reported in newspapers that are hostile to everything Europe stands for and that dismiss such basic rights as having a rest break as 'red tape'.

The new gains in employment law are why we have produced this third edition of *Your Rights at Work*. Changes in the law have brought new rights, and have made small but important changes to older rights. There are whole new issues such as e-mail privacy that hardly registered when we were producing the first edition. Rights that were relatively new for the first edition have since got better, such as the increase in annual holiday entitlement. This is not to say that there is no room for improvement. Sadly, too often the answer to 'Surely my employer can't do that!' is 'Yes, they can.'

Naturally we believe that people are better off at work if they can call on a union to help if something goes wrong. Many problems affect far more than one person, and are therefore best raised collectively with an employer. Taking legal action is very difficult without expert advice of the kind that unions can provide. But we hope this book will be useful to non-union members – and even employers – as well.

It is important to understand what this book is and what it isn't. Our purpose is to provide a general introduction to your rights at work, but it is not a legal textbook. To keep things relatively clear we have had to simplify some issues. We have not covered some situations or exemptions that affect only a very few people at work.

You cannot rely on this book therefore as expert legal advice that covers your situation. What it aims to do is explain the general requirements of the law in a way that can tell anyone with a problem whether it is worthwhile taking further advice.

As we write, we already know of some changes to employment law that are in the pipeline, though not their detailed shape. New test cases or European judgements can change how a well-established law is interpreted overnight. You should always take detailed advice on your own situation, not rely on what is in this book.

One difference between the first and later editions of this book is that we have now launched workSMART, the TUC world of work website. This contains up-to-date information not just on employment rights but on health and safety and pensions as well. For those wanting to join a union, it also features a union finder that can help identify the most appropriate union. You can find workSMART at www.worksmart. org.uk. One further change in this edition is that we have dropped the chapter on pensions. This is both because it is such a complex area that it is hard to deal with it in the short space of a chapter and because big changes are about to be made to the pensions system.

Throughout the book you will find some case studies of real tribunal and court studies. These are based on real cases, and employment law experts will no doubt recognize some of them. We have, however, simplified them where necessary, and changed the names involved. You will also find references to amounts of money, such as the current level of the minimum wage or the earnings limit for National Insurance contributions. The figures given are for 2007, but may well have been uprated by the time you read this. Normally, figures go up a few per cent a year, often in line with inflation.

Many TUC staff have contributed to the various editions of this book over the years, and they are too numerous to thank individually, but I would like to record the work of barrister Catrin Lewis in the revision of this edition.

Brendan Barber
TUC General Secretary

www.rmt.org.uk

Fighting for transport workers' rights

Trade union rights are <u>human</u> rights

Support the Trade Union Freedom Bill

Bob Crow
General Secretary

John Leach
President

Freephone members' helpline 0800 376 3706

Introduction

Your basic rights

Everyone at work is protected by a series of basic legal rights – some old and some new. Some protect you against the worst kinds of exploitation and unfair treatment. Some give you positive rights that provide some choice, and some voice, in your working life. And some are there to ensure your employer keeps their side of the basic bargain at the heart of any job – you work and in return you get paid and receive other benefits.

Most large employers are careful that their general employment practices stay within the law. If your employer is large enough to have a dedicated personnel or human resources section, then they should have the expertise that ensures they know their legal obligations. But that does not mean that everyone in the organization will always follow company policy.

And in any case there are still good and bad large employers. Many offer terms and conditions well in advance of the legal minimum. They know that treating their staff well and giving them a real say in the way that they do their work makes for a more productive workforce. Others, particularly those with many low- paid jobs, may simply want to stay just on the right side of the law. These are the employers who describe the most modest advances in employee rights as red tape and burdens on business.

Many small firms are good employers. Small business organizations often say that their staff are treated like part of the family. This is no doubt true in the best organizations, even if not every family is always a picture of perfect happiness. But others are not good employers. Sometimes this is because they depend on poor wages and conditions for the success of their business. In Britain today there are still sweatshops that Dickens would recognize.

Many more get into difficulties simply because they do not know their legal obligations as employers, or do not know how to respond to a difficult situation. Even though Employment Tribunals do not expect them to have the same formal procedures as large firms, small businesses often end up losing cases because they simply do not have any procedures for resolving disputes or problems at work, or know how to set them up if needed. This though, is no excuse, and from April 2004 all employers have been obliged to have basic procedures in place.

Issues covered by the law

Even in the best-run organizations things can go wrong. You can end up being bullied by your manager even though your employer has an anti-bullying policy. It may be that the behaviour of one of your colleagues is beginning to look like sexual harassment. Even in organizations with good health and safety records, you may be the unlucky one who does have a bad accident. Stress is on the increase everywhere.

Rapid economic change has led to many being made redundant in recent years. If you are young, skilled and live in the South East then this may be only a temporary setback to your career. For older employees it can be devastating. Many jobs have always been insecure, but fewer and fewer jobs can now be said to be secure for life.

You may be falsely accused of wrongdoing, or a minor infringement of rules may be blown up into an excuse to dismiss you. You may be tempted to walk away, but you will still need a reference.

Becoming a parent probably puts more strain on your working life than anything else does. New rights to unpaid parental leave and paid paternity leave have been added to long-established maternity provision, which has also got better in recent years.

Getting a proper balance between work and the rest of your life can be an issue for anyone. British workers work the longest hours in Europe. Some need the overtime. But many white-collar workers, who do not get overtime, are trapped in an increasingly US-style long-hours culture – where the first one home's a wimp and the number of hours you spend at your desk (whether you are working productively or not) is taken as a measure of your commitment.

Discrimination is still rife at work in Britain today. The Macpherson Report, conducted in the wake of Stephen Lawrence's murder, not only had some harsh things to say about the Metropolitan Police but established a new definition of institutional racism. Men are still paid more than women. Disabled workers are now protected to some extent against discrimination, but face enormous difficulties getting a job.

All of these are issues where the law may be able to help you, or where you need to know what the law says. Everyone at work should have a basic knowledge of employment law.

What you might get from legal action

Not every employment dispute will, or should, end up in a court of law or require lawyers to get involved. Every so often you may read in the papers of a case where someone has won, if not quite a lottery-sized payout, then at least a substantial amount of money. But these cases are very much the exception. Awards are normally much smaller, and going to court, even the more informal Employment Tribunals that hear many work-related cases, can still be traumatic. If you need to buy your own legal advice, it can also be expensive, and there is no legal aid for representation at Employment Tribunals.

This book is not, therefore, about how to win a jackpot at an Employment Tribunal – you have probably more chance with a lottery ticket. Nor do we advise that you should always go down the legal road to resolving problems at work. In most circumstances, except perhaps when you have lost your job, it should always be seen as a last resort.

But a simple knowledge of where you stand legally can often help resolve issues informally at an early stage. Simply dropping a hint that you are thinking of getting advice about early stages of RSI (Repetitive Strain Injury) can often be an effective way of getting a better chair and workstation. In general, letting your employer know that you have rights can often lead to a swift improvement, particularly if your employer is ignorant of the law.

Unions and employment rights

Resolving disputes is normally much easier in a company where unions are recognized. Nearly every basic recognition agreement between a union and an employer will have ways of resolving both individual and collective grievances. There will be proper procedures for dealing with disciplinary issues. This is sensible for both employers and employees. Companies, these days, are fond of asserting in their annual reports that their staff are their greatest asset. Ensuring they have ways of raising problems with a real expectation that they will be solved is one relatively modest way of demonstrating that in practice.

Reading some newspapers, you might conclude that unions are quick to bring tribunal cases. In fact the opposite is true. Most tribunal cases come from non-union companies, particularly small employers. This is because they do not have the kind of procedures needed to ensure that disputes and grievances can be settled properly in-house or are ignorant of such basic employee protection as not being able to sack someone because she is pregnant.

How to raise an issue

It can be much more difficult to raise an issue in a non-union workplace. While you do have legal rights that can be enforced, it does not mean that this will be easy. The employment relationship is one-sided. If your employer wants to treat you badly because you have tried to raise a problem issue, then as long as they do it relatively subtly then they will probably get away with it. On the other hand it may be that your employer was completely unaware of the problem and is happy to deal with it informally. You must make your own judgement about how, or even whether, you raise an issue.

If you are not the only one with a grievance then there is strength in numbers. You and your colleagues should consider joining a union. There are new rights that allow union officers to represent you with your employer, even if they do not recognize a union, and if there is sufficient support then they must recognize and deal properly with your union (see Chapter 5).

Sometimes round robins or petitions have persuaded an employer that there is widespread dissatisfaction and they need to take action. In other cases an anonymous letter, which includes a government publication, making it clear that the employer could be in legal difficulties, can bring about change. You might think about sending a delegation to your employer, with very clear backing from the rest of the workforce. Some issues – such as the minimum wage or health and safety issues – can be discussed with an official body, and it can then raise problems with your employer without revealing who tipped it off in the first place.

If the worst comes to the worst you may be able to walk out of your job and claim what is known as 'constructive dismissal'. In other words you persuade an Employment Tribunal that your employer may not have formally sacked you, but they still forced you out of your job. However, these claims are quite difficult to win and you should carefully read Chapter 7 and take further advice. But of course if you have already been unfairly sacked then you may have little to lose by taking action.

Even if you take an action, and win it, it may still be an unpleasant and difficult experience. While many tribunal cases are over quickly, some can drag out or end up going through lengthy appeal stages. You may end up being cross-examined by an aggressive lawyer for your employer with the aim of showing you in the worst possible light. If it's a case with a media angle, this could be reported in the papers.

In general we think people should stand up for their rights. Bad employers do need tackling. A long and difficult case may end up clarifying the law, and thus help thousands of other people. But you should be aware of both the potential benefits *and* the downsides of taking any action. You should always talk this through very carefully with an adviser before committing yourself to a course of action that could bring you into conflict with your employer.

As well as trade unions, there are many other advice agencies that may be able to help, such as your local Citizens' Advice Bureau or law centre. There are a range of telephone helplines – some run by voluntary groups set up to deal with particular problems and others by official or publicly funded groups, such as ACAS. In addition to its 'Know Your Rights Line', the TUC has its own workSMART website, www.worksmart.org.uk, which provides up-to-date information on employment rights, and can point you in the right direction if you want to know which union you should join. These resources are all listed at the end of the book.

Employment law

In a book like this, we can only provide a general introduction to employment law. Inevitably we have had to simplify many issues. The law may even have changed since this book was written. As we will stress many times, you always need to take detailed advice about your particular circumstances. The rest of this chapter gives a basic introduction to your rights at work and explains some of the key concepts in employment law.

The first important thing to understand is the difference between an employee and a worker. In everyday conversation employee is probably just a slightly posh term for a worker, but in law they are quite different concepts. Employees have many more rights than workers. To understand the difference, you need to understand the nature of the contract between you and your employer, which we explain on pages 8–9.

There are two different kinds of right. There is a basic floor of legal protection that every employee enjoys. In addition, because there is a contract between you and your employer – you work and in return they pay you – most people have additional rights provided by this contract.

The law does not just protect you from a bad or unfair employer; it also imposes duties on you and allows your employer to take action against you if you are guilty of misconduct.

Statutory rights

The basic rights that provide a minimum floor for everyone derive from the law of the land and are known as statutory rights. These normally come either from a government initiative, like the minimum wage, or from Europe, like the working time directive.

The new employment rights such as parental leave that come from Europe are the result of negotiations between employers and unions at the European level. But the European directives that result from this process still need to be turned into UK law. This will normally be done through a set of legally binding regulations.

But while parliament makes new laws, the courts have to interpret them. Although laws are intended to be precise, they can never cover every eventuality. Inevitably they will contain words that are a matter of opinion; for example, 'reasonable' is frequently found in employment law, and an employer's definition of reasonable may not be the same as an employee's they have just sacked.

Over time the courts will hear enough cases that require them to decide how to apply words like 'reasonable' for a body of what lawyers call 'case law' to develop. This makes it much easier to predict how a case will go when it gets to court, as normally the courts will want to make decisions in line with previous similar cases. Sometimes, however, a particular case will set an important new legal precedent, and will end up going through every possible appeal stage (see Chapter 8).

But much employment law is relatively new, and there have not yet been many court cases. It is sometimes hard therefore to give precise guidance on how some new rights will be interpreted by the courts. And while the legal system is heavily based on case law, sometimes the courts can be persuaded to look again at an issue.

Another legal route sometimes used in employment law challenges whether the government has properly put European directives into UK law. European directives are often quite broadly drawn because they need to apply across the countries that make up the European Union, with all their different legal systems and industrial relations traditions. But while there is usually room for flexibility in some areas, sometimes a case will be brought using the argument that the UK government has not properly implemented a European directive.

Such cases can end up in the European Court of Justice – the European Union's court where European law is normally settled. An example of this process was the landmark case that found that employers could not exclude part-time workers from company pension schemes. The court ruled that this was sex discrimination as part-time workers are more likely than full-time workers to be women. The TUC also successfully challenged the government's parental leave rules in this way.

Contractual rights

The second types of employment right you enjoy are called contractual rights, so termed because they flow from the contract between you and your employer. Your employment contract is a personal, legal agreement that governs your relationship with your employer.

Employment contracts are usually written down, and you will normally be given one before or when you start work. But even if you are not given a written contract, the courts will rule that a contract exists simply because you are being paid in return for working. Whether written or not, your contract will oblige your employer to pay you for work or services performed, to provide work for you, provide a safe working environment and behave in a 'reasonable' manner.

You are obliged to 'serve' (or to work or perform a service), to be 'obedient', to be competent and careful and act in good faith. These old-fashioned terms are still used in the courts. They are called 'implied' terms, because they are not necessarily written into the contract but are assumed by the courts to exist in any relationship between an employer and an employee or worker.

If you have a written contract then it will also include other terms that regulate the relationship you have with your employer. It is likely to include how much you will be paid, what notice of dismissal your employer must give you, and your entitlement to holidays. Because they are written down, unlike the implied terms, they are called 'express' terms.

Although these express terms are in addition to your statutory rights, they do impact on your more general legal rights. This is because they define the kind of employment relationship you have with your employer. As the next section explains, there are different types of relationship between employer and employed and each carries different entitlements to statutory rights.

Worker or employee?

Whether you are a worker or an employee depends upon the contractual relationship you have with your employer. Every year court cases hang on this distinction, and unfortunately there is no easy definition. As the courts cannot agree on a simple test, we can only provide a rough rule of thumb.

If your employer provides work for you on a regular basis, says when and where it is to be done, supplies the tools or other equipment and pays tax and National Insurance on your behalf then you are almost certainly an employee.

If, on the other hand, you decide when you will work, make your own sickness and holiday arrangements and pay your own tax and National Insurance you are probably a self-employed person contracted to provide a service to the employer. This means you are a worker, not an employee. To introduce some more legal jargon, the relationship you have with your employer is a 'contract for services' rather than a 'contract of employment'.

Sometimes your employer will pay your tax and National Insurance but only ask you to come to work when work is available, for example, on a seasonal basis. In this situation, it is likely that you are a 'casual' worker.

It may be that you are given a contract of employment that states that you will only be required to come in when work is available. When it is not, you will not be paid. Some days you will not work at all, although you have to be available to work if your employer calls you. This sort of contract is commonly called a 'zero hours contract'. In this situation, you are an employee, but with no right to work (or pay, except for when you work).

Most people will clearly fit into one of these categories, but if you do not and fall between them then it might not be possible to definitively say which you are without a court or tribunal case. This is clearly a major problem, as many statutory rights, for example, the right to redundancy pay, only apply to employees.

Many people are happy to be self-employed and some occupations by their nature – such as journalism – are likely to have a significant proportion of self-employed workers. But some unscrupulous employers deliberately try to prevent the people who work for them becoming employees so that they do not enjoy proper employment protection. The government has taken powers to regulate this in the Employment Relations Act 1999, but this has yet to make much difference.

A further confusion is that HM Revenue & Customs uses its own stricter definitions to guard against bogus self-employment being used as a tax dodge. It is perfectly possible therefore to be taxed as an employee, but to be legally self-employed. You cannot therefore use your tax status as a guide to your employment status. There is an obvious degree of unfairness here. The law allows an employer to get away with denying you employment rights, but still makes sure you do not get the more favourable tax treatment enjoyed by the self-employed.

If the law ever gets involved in defining your employment status then the courts will look at all relevant factors. Remember that your own views on whether or not you are self-employed may not be the same as those of your employer, or of the courts.

As we said at the start of this section there are a lot of grey areas here. Take for example someone who works as a cleaner in private households, working every Monday for one family, every Tuesday for another and so on. If you are in this position it is possible to be either self-employed or an employee of each family for whom you work. If you are paid by the hour, work set hours and only use cleaning tools provided by each family then you are probably employed.

If the working arrangement is more flexible then you may very well be self-employed. Say you clean the house and go when you've finished, with some choice about when you do it, with no set hours, use your own tools and are free to send a friend instead. It is pretty clear here that you are being paid to perform a service, rather than being given a job. You are still a worker, but you are not an employee.

So, if you are an employee you have a 'contract of employment' with your employer. Normally this will be written down, but if it is not then the courts will still consider that a contract exists between you and your employer. If necessary they will rule on your contractual rights by looking at what your employer may have said to you, the custom and practice established since your employment began and anything else that can help them establish the contractual relationship between you and your employer.

If you are an employee you will also enjoy the statutory rights described throughout this book, although many only start after you have worked for your employer for a qualifying period – for example, one year for protection against unfair dismissal.

If you are a worker, but not an employee, then you do not have a contract of employment. It is likely that instead you have 'a contract for services'. You still enjoy some statutory rights, for example, the minimum wage, but you will miss out on many others. There is more about your contract in the next chapter.

1

Starting a job

The law starts to protect you as soon as you apply for a job. When you start work you gain more protection, and other rights kick in the longer you work for your employer.

Applying for and getting a job

You have some rights as soon as you apply for a job. When drawing up a shortlist or appointing the successful candidate, your employer must not discriminate against you because of your sex, race, age, sexuality, religion or disability. Nor can an employer rule you out because you are a member of a trade union or have a record of activity as a trade union member. It is also likely that employers will soon be effectively banned from asking you about your pension arrangements.

At some stage during the appointments process, your prospective employer is likely to ask for a reference. This is normally a statement from your previous employer or from your school or college saying that in their opinion you would be able to do the job. If the reference turns out to be inaccurate it could, in some circumstances, provide your employer with grounds to dismiss you. There have also been cases where employers have challenged reference providers and accused them of giving an over-favourable reference in order to get rid of someone.

Most application forms are clear that if you are found to have lied when filling in the form you will be liable to dismissal. In the past, few employers have bothered to check the facts on an application form but companies are now being established that will check CVs and application forms for dishonesty, such as 'exaggerating' educational qualifications. This must be done with your agreement, but in reality there is not much of a choice as you will be very unlikely to be considered for the job if you refuse. Honesty is, therefore, the best policy, but there are many ways of presenting your achievements in the best possible light and many books will provide tips.

As well as asking whether they can check your references with an agency, an employer may ask you to take a drugs test. Again you can refuse, but an employer can make that refusal the grounds for not giving you the job. This would only be illegal if they were treating different applicants in different ways based on one of the illegal forms of discrimination. If, for example, only black applicants with dreadlocks were being asked to take a drugs test, then this would be illegal racial discrimination.

Under the Immigration and Asylum Act 1996 your employer must ask you for your National Insurance number or some other evidence that you have a legal right to work in the UK. Employers must make this check for all new employees. If they limited it to one racial group or chose people they thought had a foreign name they would be guilty of racial discrimination.

Employers may ask you about any criminal convictions you have. But you do not have to reveal them if they are 'spent'. This means they happened long enough ago for the Rehabilitation of Offenders Act 1974 to allow you to keep them secret. For more information contact the National Association for the Care and Resettlement of Offenders (NACRO) whose contact details are included in Chapter 9.

If you want to work with children or vulnerable adults, you will need to provide a certificate of 'Disclosure'. This is an official document, which you get from the Criminal Records Bureau, that lists any relevant past convictions. Your prospective employer must check with the police that you have no convictions involving children. If you are not working with vulnerable people, you only need to tell your employer about unspent criminal convictions if you are asked.

When you accept a job offer

As soon as you have been offered a job and have accepted it, there is a basic legal contract between you and the employer, even if you have received nothing in writing. This works two ways. Firstly, it means that your employer has promised you a job. If the offer is withdrawn it may be possible to sue your prospective employer, particularly if you have suffered loss because you have left your previous job. Breaking a contract is known as a breach of contract in legal jargon. If a court decides that your contract has been breached, it can order your employer to pay you 'damages' or compensation. Secondly, it means that you have accepted the terms that are offered.

Contractual rights

You may not be given a document called 'a contract of employment'. Instead you might be given something called a staff handbook or a similar title. If you are, you may find some small print that says which sections are part of your contract of employment and therefore legally binding, and which bits are there simply for information. For example, the disciplinary and holiday arrangements are likely to be part of your contract of employment, but the location of coffee machines in your workplace is not.

Your contract cannot remove or reduce your statutory rights. Even if you sign a contract in which you agree to receive less than the minimum wage or sign away your rights to claim unfair dismissal, you are still protected. If a case went to court, any clause that undercut your legal rights would be struck out as 'void'.

In the Introduction we looked at the difference between implied terms – those assumed by the court to be in any contract of employment; and express terms – those written down. But there are other ways you can gain contractual rights. If you work for an employer who recognizes a trade union and negotiates with the union about the terms and conditions enjoyed by you or people doing your job, then your contract can be changed as a result of an employer–union agreement. These changes apply whether or not you are a member of the union as long as the recognition agreement covers workers on your grade or doing your job. Normally, any change to a contract agreed as a result of union negotiations will be an improvement, but there will often be a trade-off involved – more time off and better pay for agreeing to work more flexible hours, for example.

The other way you can gain contractual rights is through what is called 'custom and practice'. This means that if your employer has done something for some time – for example, laundering staff uniforms – you would have a reasonable expectation that this would continue, and if it were to stop, you should be notified in advance.

All contracts work two ways, and your contract of employment can also put obligations on you. It may 'restrain' what you can do. For example, it might say you cannot work for a rival company for six months after leaving your current job. There may be confidentiality clauses that leave you open to legal action if you pass on sensitive information to others, although the law provides protection for whistle-blowers (see pages 27–29), so if you tell commercial secrets to a rival then you could end up in court, but if you tell a watchdog about a pollution cover-up then you will be safe if you have followed the right procedures.

Frustrated

Kevin Evans had been employed as one of two night service fitters. In April 1974, Kevin contracted industrial dermatitis and was off sick. He periodically sent in sickness certificates. In August 1974, the employer took on a replacement, but Kevin was not formally dismissed. In January 1976, Kevin recovered and turned up for work. But his boss told him there was no work for him, and gave him his P45. Kevin claimed unfair dismissal.

But Kevin lost. The tribunal ruled that his contract of employment had come to an end by frustration. This is a somewhat obscure legal term, but can crop up in contract of employment cases. Frustration occurs when some 'reasonably unforeseeable event' takes place that makes the contract impossible or unlawful to perform, or radically different from what the parties originally intended. It means the contract is no longer in operation. And as there is now no contract of employment, there is no job from which you can be dismissed.

Because frustration means there is no possibility of unfair dismissal, employers have sometimes found it an attractive argument to use in tribunal cases. Tribunals have recognized that a finding of frustration of contract removes the right to claim unfair dismissal, and have therefore tended to impose a high onus of proof on employers who claim a contract of employment has been frustrated. The matters a tribunal would take into account in deciding that a contract has been frustrated include:

■ length of previous employment;
■ expected future duration of employment;
■ nature of the job;
■ employer's need for the job to be done and the need for a replacement to do it;
■ the risk to the employer of acquiring employment protection obligations towards a replacement employee;
■ whether an employee has continued to be paid;
■ the acts and statements of the employer in relation to the employment (in other words, is there any evidence that

the employer has acted as if the contract is still in existence);
■ whether a reasonable employer could be expected to wait any longer for the employee to return.

It is important to note that there is no set time after which a contract is frustrated, and contracts have been found to run for nearly two years even though the employee had not done any work.

Your contract may also set out benefits other than your pay, such as details of your pension or company car. It may set out your grading system and provide information on increments, performance review, performance-related pay and promotion. In general if you work for a large company you are likely to get a detailed contract of employment that will cover most of the issues likely to arise between an employer and employee. If you work for a smaller company, you may have a much more limited contract, even if you have a generally fair employer.

Both you and your employer are legally bound by the terms of your contract and by statutory laws. If you think your employer has broken the terms of your contract or broken a statutory law, you may be able to pursue a claim. There is a section on dealing with disputes about your contract in Chapter 5.

If you break the terms of your contract, this may be treated as a disciplinary matter by your employer, or in extreme circumstances could allow them to sue you, almost certainly after dismissing you as well. Of course if you have already left your job then a court case is the only option open to your former employer.

Contracts can be written in a way that allows your employer to make changes in your conditions. For example, your contract may state that you would normally work Mondays to Fridays but there may be times when you will be required to work on a Saturday. If your employer wants to change the terms of your contract, they should give you a statement setting out the new conditions and asking you to accept them.

If you do not agree, and do not in practice accept them, and your employer ignores this, then they are likely to be in breach of contract. This means that if the change is fundamental – such as changing your retirement age or cutting your wages – you can sue in the civil courts. If the court finds in your favour, it can order your employer to restore the original terms of your contract. But you will not succeed if the change is minor (see Chapter 6 for more on this).

Your 'written statement of employment particulars'

No later than two months after you have started your new job, you are entitled to a 'written statement of employment particulars'. This is a statement setting out your basic employment conditions. The written statement must include:

- your name and the name of your employer;
- the date when your employment started;
- your rate of pay (which must be at least at the rate of the national minimum wage), when you will be paid and how your pay has been calculated;
- your hours of work and your holiday entitlement, including public holidays (both of these must provide the maximum/minimum given under the Working Time Regulations);
- the title or description of your job and your place of work (this can state that you may be required to work in different locations);
- your notice period;
- the employer's grievance and disciplinary procedures (see pages 125–134).

You must also be informed in the statement whether your employment is permanent or for a fixed term. A fixed term contract will specify when your employment will cease but your employer must still give you the required notice before your leaving date.

There are new laws in place on fixed term contracts. If you have one, your employer must not treat you less well than equivalent permanent employees. Your employer cannot keep on renewing your fixed term contract indefinitely; after four years of continuous service you will legally be considered permanent.

You should also be given details of any agreement with a union about your terms and conditions (see above) and details of any requirement to work outside the UK. The statement can refer to other documents that you may have been given – for example, a staff handbook, which includes information about things such as your pension (if there is one).

If you have already been given a contract of employment that covers everything that is required to be in your written statement, it will count as your written statement. Strictly speaking, your written statement is not a contract of employment but it can be used as evidence of your pay and conditions in any legal proceedings or for social security purposes.

You are also entitled to a written statement about your pay with, or before, your first wage packet or pay cheque. This is known as an 'itemized pay statement' (see Chapter 2 for more details of what this should include).

Other rights at work

There are many other rights at work. Some start on your first day of employment, others only after you have been in your job some time. The rest of this chapter lists the most important ones. Some only apply in practice to a small number of people or deal with very specific situations. We will mention many of them here, but you will need to go elsewhere for more detailed advice. Rights that everyone at work needs to know about are listed here and dealt with in more detail in later chapters. The chapter concludes with a list of rights and how long you have to wait before you are entitled to them.

Time off for public and workforce duties

All employees are entitled to reasonable unpaid time off to perform various public duties, including serving as a magistrate or a local authority councillor. Your contract of employment may give you a right to paid time off for such duties. Trade union representatives (where unions are recognized), Union Learning representatives, company pension fund trustees and designated health and safety representatives are also entitled to paid time off work to fulfil their duties.

Losing or leaving your job

Both you and your employer are entitled to a minimum period of notice of termination of employment. After one month's employment, you must give your employer at least one week's notice. Your employer must give you at least one week's notice for every year you have worked for them up to a maximum of 12 weeks, unless you are guilty of gross misconduct (for more about this see Chapter 5).

Once you have had your job for at least a year, you can ask for a written statement of reasons for your dismissal. You should be given one automatically if you get the sack while you are pregnant or on maternity leave, even if you have only just started your job. You are protected against unfair dismissal after a year's service, and in some special circumstances as soon as you have started a job (see Chapter 7).

Public and bank holidays

Contrary to popular belief, you have no statutory right to be off work on public or bank holidays. Your contract may give you that right, however. If it does and you are required to work on a public holiday, you may have something in your contract that provides for extra pay or time off in lieu. Your employer may count time off on public or bank holidays as part of your holiday entitlement. It is legal for such days off to count towards your statutory annual leave under the Working Time Regulations (see Chapter 3), but annual leave entitlements are being raised in two stages so that UK employees get the European minimum of four weeks, plus eight days in addition to reflect UK public holidays. This followed a long union campaign to crack down on employers who were counting bank holidays like Christmas Day against the four-week entitlement.

Transfer of a business

If your company is taken over by another one, or if you work for a public authority and your job is transferred to a private company, your terms and conditions of employment transfer automatically to the new company. In other words, whatever is provided for in your contract continues and you will be counted as having continuity of employment. So, for example, you do not have to work another year before you can claim unfair dismissal.

You have the right to object to your contract being transferred to another company. But this can be dangerous, as it can be treated as you resigning. If you do object, but continue working for the new owner, the courts are likely to say that you have accepted the new contract. However, if you do not object at the time of transfer but walk out once you have started because there has been a substantial change for the worse in your working conditions, then you have the right to claim unfair dismissal and may also have a claim for constructive dismissal (see Chapter 7). But walking out is always risky and you should take advice before doing this.

If you are dismissed by either your old or new employer simply because of the change in ownership then the dismissal is automatically unfair and you could claim at an Employment Tribunal. If, as is often unfortunately the case, takeovers and transfers do lead to job losses, then your employer must follow the procedures for redundancy in Chapter 7.

'Transfers of undertakings', as this area of employment law is known, is particularly complex. European law, which has been recently revised, and UK law are both involved. If you have a problem in this area, you will need good legal advice. A union or advice agency will be able to help.

Sunday working

Special protection has been introduced for some groups of workers when activities that were once prohibited on Sundays have been liberalized in recent years. These include shop workers and people who work in betting – either at racetracks or licensed betting offices. The aim was to allow people working in those sectors who did not want to work on Sundays to resist any employer pressure to start to do so.

You do not have this protection, however, if you have agreed a contract of employment that says you will work on Sundays. It is likely that staff taken on since the change of the law will have contracts that include Sunday working, but if you do not, or started work before the law changed, then you are protected. This means your employer cannot dismiss you, single you out for redundancy or punish you in any way for refusing to work on Sundays. You can get more information on this from your union or from the Department for Business, Enterprise and Regulatory Reform (see addresses section in Chapter 9).

You only have special protection, however, if you work in one of these occupations. For everyone else Sunday is just another day of the week. Although in many jobs overtime payments or premiums are available for working on Sundays, there is no legal right to them, although they may be part of your contract of employment.

Guarantee payments

If you are laid off for some reason – in other words, if there is no work for you on a particular day and you are sent home – you are entitled to a 'guarantee payment' for up to five days in any three-month period. To get a guarantee payment, you must have worked for your employer for at least one month continuously, you must not have refused unreasonably to do other work offered by your employer, and the lay-off must not be because of a strike.

You do not have to be paid your contractual pay, unless your contract says that you will be paid if you are laid off, but you have to be paid the statutory minimum, which is currently £19.60 a day. If there is union recognition then better rates may well have been negotiated. The legal minimum is normally uprated in line with inflation each year, so may be a little more by the time you read this.

Insolvency of your employer

If your employer goes bust and cannot pay your wages, the state will make up at least some of your lost pay. You can claim what you have lost up to a maximum of £310 a week for up to eight weeks. This maximum is normally uprated in line with inflation each year. As well as your basic wages you can claim up to six weeks' holiday pay, any company pension and up to 12 weeks' notice pay due to you. You must apply to what is known as the employer's representative, usually the liquidator or receiver. He or she will give you a form that you must complete and send to the address shown on the form. You will then receive payment.

Suspension on medical grounds

Your employer may suspend you from work for health and safety reasons when you are ill. This may be because your employer thinks you are likely to do damage to yourself or your fellow employees if you worked. If this happens, you are entitled to up to 26 weeks' pay as long as you have worked for your employer continuously for one month and you make the claim within three months of the suspension starting. You must not refuse a reasonable offer of alternative work. The grounds for claiming medical suspension are strictly applied so you should get advice if you think this applies to you. You make your claim to an Employment Tribunal if your employer is not paying you, or you think they are not paying you the right amount.

Agency workers

All agency workers have some basic protection under the 1973 Employment Agencies Act. The government has recently improved this. If you are working for an employment agency you may or may not legally be an employee. At the very least you will be a worker, hired out to a company by the agency to perform a service. But the largest employment 'agencies' in the UK are not actually agencies in the strictest legal sense but businesses. They tend to employ their staff directly, as employees. Whether or not you are an employee, agency workers still have some basic rights. All agency workers:

■ are covered by health and safety law, where the agency has a responsibility not to place you in a job for which you are not appropriately qualified and the hiring company is generally responsible for providing a healthy and safe working environment for you (see Chapter 5);
■ are covered by discrimination law, which covers both the agency and the hiring company (see Chapter 6);
■ are entitled to be paid the minimum wage (see Chapter 2);
■ are entitled not to work more than an average of 48 hours a week, unless you sign an agreement with the agency saying that you are willing to work longer hours (see Chapter 3);
■ should receive four weeks' paid annual leave once you have worked for 13 weeks, increasing to four weeks and four days from 1 October 2007 and then to five weeks and three days from 1 April 2009.

Some agencies have been getting round this by saying that your pay includes holiday pay and that they therefore do not have to pay extra if you take a break, but a recent European Court ruling makes clear that this is not allowed (with only some minor exceptions, mainly to deal with transitional arrangements for people paid this way in the past). It is always worth shopping around to see which agency will give you the best deal. If you are only looking for a short-term stopgap then holiday pay may not matter, but if you are looking to temp for some time or fear that you may not get a longer-term job, then ask about holiday rights and pay.

As an agency worker you may also be entitled to Statutory Maternity Pay and Statutory Sick Pay, depending on your earnings and how long you have worked for the agency. You are allowed to join a union and a few agencies encourage their workers to do so.

If you are working as an agency worker, and the hiring company offers you a permanent job, you are likely to be expected to work out a period of notice in the job as an agency temp before becoming a permanent employee of the company. Alternatively, the company may have to pay the agency a sum in lieu of notice. Any such arrangements have to be explained to you when you sign on with the agency.

There are other basic protections for agency workers:

■ You have the right to be paid by your agency, on the agreed day, even if the hiring company has not paid the agency.

■ You must be consulted before any changes are made to your contract or the terms under which you work.

■ Different rules apply in the entertainment industry. For example, it is legal to charge you a fee for trying to find you a job. If you are a musician, a performer, or work in some other capacity in the entertainment business through an agency – for example, as a camera operator – you should check what the rules are (see Chapter 9 for useful addresses). The entertainment industry is well unionized, and the unions in this sector can give detailed advice to their members.

As this edition was being updated, discussions were going on in Europe about increased protection for agency workers but they have provoked considerable controversy and may not result in significant change. Even if new rules are agreed, they are unlikely to be implemented immediately.

Trade union rights

Everyone in the UK has the right to join a trade union. Joining a trade union is a private matter and you do not have to tell your employer that you have joined. On the other hand, you do not have to join a trade union and you have legal protection in the unlikely event that you are discriminated against for not joining one.

You are free to join any union, or unions, which you choose. However, it makes sense to join a trade union that is already active in your workplace. If it has recognition rights with your employer then it will be in a strong position to look after you at work, accompany you if you have to go to a disciplinary hearing and so on. You will also have a say in any negotiations between the union and your employer.

But even if there is no union recognized, a union can still offer help, advice and representation. Even if your employer says that they do not like unions and do not want you to join one, you can join without them finding out. Even if your employer finds out, they must not treat you differently as a result. It is illegal for an employer to discriminate on grounds of trade union membership or activity.

If there is a collective agreement with a union in your workplace, you may be entitled to time off for attending meetings organized by the union. You would also get time off for union duties if you volunteered to become a union representative in your workplace. For details about how to join a union, see Chapter 9, 'Further information', at the back of the book.

You are also protected against unfair dismissal for going on strike, as long as the strike is a legal one, that is, the union has held a ballot and met other legal conditions before calling you out. You are protected for the first 12 weeks of the strike.

'Whistle-blowing'

Whistle-blowing is when an individual reports to the authorities something seriously wrong or illegal taking place in the organization for which he or she works. The Public Interest Disclosure Act 1998 provided new rights for staff who raise genuine concerns over a range of misconduct and malpractice issues. These rights cover virtually all workers, including those employed on 'worker' contracts or as contractors, trainees, agency staff or home workers, and all health professionals. However, they do not cover volunteers, the armed forces or police officers.

A worker who blows the whistle will be protected if the disclosure is both made in good faith and concerns illegal activities, including crimes, theft or fraud, or actions that endanger staff, customers or the local community. In particular, the Act extends protection to all individuals who raise genuine concerns about health, safety or environmental risks.

The law expects you to use the procedures at your workplace before you take the problem to an outside body, except in the most serious cases. You can do this by using your workplace grievance procedure or by going to a senior manager or a manager other than your own. If there is a union in your workplace then talk to your union representative first. If raising the issue at work fails to resolve the situation properly, you can go to the appropriate official body, for example the Health and Safety Executive, the Serious Fraud Office, HM Revenue & Customs or the Audit Commission. If you work for a quango or in the NHS, it may be possible to raise the issue with the relevant government minister, but you should get advice first.

Only in very exceptional cases should an individual make wider disclosures, for example to MPs or the police. You will only get protection in such cases if the issue at stake is exceptionally serious – for example, a person's life is at risk – and you believe that the situation has not been dealt with properly when you raised it internally or with the appropriate agency. You should definitely consider getting advice from your union or a legal adviser before doing so. Public Concern at Work can offer practical help and advice on whistle-blowing issues. Contact details are given in Chapter 9.

If you are dismissed or victimized after raising concerns internally, you can take a claim for reinstatement or compensation to an Employment Tribunal. There is no qualifying period for bringing such a claim, and compensation awards are unlimited, although they will in practice be based on your pay, how long you have worked with your employer, your future employment prospects and so on. Confidentiality clauses, such as gagging clauses in your employment contract, that conflict with the Act will not be legally binding. It is important to note, however, that you will not normally be protected for whistleblowing to the media. In that situation you will also be at risk from a slander or libel action brought against you by your employer. This will effectively gag you, even if you are right, and involve you in legal costs, although reputable journalists will endeavour to protect their sources.

The Data Protection Act

Privacy at work is becoming more of an issue every day. New technology allows employers to collect substantial information about their staff, while surveillance techniques in the workplace are becoming ever more sophisticated and intrusive. Snooping is now easy.

The Data Protection Act 1998 provides some important rights, which individuals should be aware of, that give employees some control over the information their employer holds on them. The Act gives all workers the right to be told about the type of information their employer holds, how that information is to be used and about anyone else with access to it. Your employer must make sure that your information is kept confidential. Only those with a legitimate reason to see data can do so, unless you have given your permission. Employers are not allowed to maintain sensitive data on you, such as information about your sexuality, race, political or religious opinions or beliefs, union membership, health and criminal offences (except those under the Children Act 1989). Employers can hold or use such sensitive data only in very limited situations, for instance where they are required to do so by law – when dealing with Statutory Sick Pay, for example.

You have the right to ask to see a copy of the information held about you by making a written request to your employer. The Data Protection Act covers data kept on both electronic and paper files. You can usually expect to see personnel files, information about worker movements and timesheets, appraisal forms and papers prepared before disciplinary procedures. Film recordings and other monitoring records are also covered in some cases. The legislation also allows you to see your references from previous employers, but not a reference provided by your current employer for a prospective employer. An employer must respond promptly to any written request to see data and can require a worker to pay a fee (up to £10) for producing the information. An employer can refuse to disclose information if releasing it would involve a breach of a duty of confidence to a third party or would involve a disproportionate effort. If your employer will not tell you what data they are keeping on you, or passes your information on to someone else without your permission, you may make a complaint to the Information Commissioner's Office (see Chapter 9 for contact details).

Monitoring at work

Monitoring is to some extent a routine part of the employer–employee relationship. Most employers make some checks on the quantity and quality of work produced by their staff, and employees will generally expect and accept this.

Some employers carry out monitoring to safeguard workers, as well as to protect their own interests or those of their customers. For example, monitoring may help ensure that workers in hazardous jobs are not at risk from unsafe working practices; in some financial services employers have legal or regulatory obligations that they can only fulfil by using some monitoring; some employees may be at risk of attack by members of the public.

However, where monitoring goes beyond just watching the performance of an individual and involves the collection, processing and storage of personal data, it needs to be done in a way that is both lawful and fair. If used in inappropriate ways or in the wrong situations, monitoring can have a negative effect on staff, intrude into their private lives, disrupt their work, and interfere with the proper relationship of mutual trust and confidence between employee and employer.

The Information Commissioner has set out guidance for employers in the Employment Practice Data Protection Code. Although the code is not a legal obligation in itself, if your employer is not adhering to it, he or she may be breaking one or more of the laws on which it is based. For more information on the code of practice and a helpful guide for employers, you can visit the website of the government Information Commissioner at www.informationcommissioner.gov.uk.

The Data Protection Act says that workplace monitoring must be justified by the benefits that the employer and others would gain from it. Therefore, the code of practice suggests that in all but the most minor cases employers carry out an 'impact assessment' when deciding if and how to use monitoring. They must also consider whether the monitoring is a proportionate response to the problem it seeks to address.

An impact assessment should:

- clearly identify the reason for the monitoring arrangement and the benefits it is likely to deliver;
- identify any likely negative effect of the monitoring on staff, including their private lives within the workplace;
- consider alternatives to monitoring, or different ways in which it might be carried out with less disruption;
- take into account the obligations that arise from monitoring;
- take into account the results of any consultation with unions or other staff representatives.

Knowledge and consent

Under the Data Protection Act, if monitoring involves the collection or other processing of personal data you should be made aware that it is being carried out and told why. Simply telling you that, for example, your e-mails may be monitored is not sufficient. You should be left with a clear understanding of when information about you is likely to be obtained, why it is being obtained and how it will be used.

Employers who have carried out a properly conducted impact assessment do not generally need the consent of individual workers. Consent is only likely to be an issue if your employer wants to collect sensitive data such as information about your sexuality, race or political opinions, and there are strict rules about this (see the section on the Data Protection Act on pages 29–30).

The Data Protection Act restricts employers from using covert audio or video monitoring in areas that workers would genuinely and reasonably expect to be private such as toilets, changing rooms or private offices.

Where video or audio monitoring takes place, staff should have specific information such as the location of cameras or microphones. This information should be available in staff handbooks, on intranets, or in other places where staff usually find out about personnel policy. Staff should be informed if significant changes are introduced. Where communications are monitored, the information may be less specific but staff should know when to expect that information about them will be collected.

The only exception to the principle of notifying staff is where an employer is justified in using covert monitoring to investigate a genuine suspicion of criminal activity or serious wrongdoing. If your employer is using this justification, they should have a clear intention to involve the police in the matter.

Covert monitoring

Covert monitoring means monitoring deliberately carried out in secret, so that the staff being monitored are unaware of it. It is hard for an employer to justify, and should be used only in very limited circumstances. Your employer must have genuine suspicions that criminal activity or malpractice is taking place, and that notifying individuals about the monitoring would prejudice its prevention or detection.

Covert monitoring must be strictly targeted at obtaining evidence within a set timeframe, and restricted to gathering evidence about the suspected malpractice. This means that it must not continue after the investigation is over, and that any other information collected during this time should be disre garded, unless it reveals something that no employer could reasonably be expected to ignore.

The code also requires employers to share information with workers, if it would have an adverse impact on them, before taking any action. Automated monitoring results can be incomplete or open to misinterpretation, and staff should be able to see – and if necessary explain or challenge – the results of monitoring.

Personal information collected through monitoring should not be used for purposes other than those for which the monitoring was introduced, unless it is clearly in the individual's interest to do so, or it reveals activity that no employer could reasonably be expected to ignore.

Monitoring e-mail and web use

Personal use of your employer's e-mail system, or the employer's web access if you are using the internet or web-based e-mail, is a privilege of your job rather than a right. Many employers use automated systems to identify unacceptable web use, flagging up or preventing access to websites that are on a 'banned' list or judged by an automatic system to be a risk.

Your employer has a duty to inform you if they are planning to systematically monitor e-mail in your workplace. Make sure you've read and understood your employer's policy on e-mail and web use. Talk to your workplace union rep if you have one, as he or she is likely to know of any cases or policies. If your employer doesn't have one, always assume the worst. Act cautiously, and ask your manager to clarify what personal use of e-mail or the web is permitted.

We believe that employees should be allowed some personal use of the internet in their own time at work, in the same way that they should have access to the phone for reasonable personal use. This is especially the case in workplaces where people regularly put in long hours. This privilege needs to be used responsibly, however, and balanced with the employer's valid interests in protecting their business's reputation.

An outline for a good electronic communications policy

To satisfy data protection requirements, a company's policy for the use of electronic communications should as a minimum:

■ set out clearly the circumstances in which employees may or may not use the employer's phone systems (including mobile phones), e-mail system and the internet for private communications;
■ make clear the extent and type of private use allowed – for example, restrictions on overseas phone calls or limits on the size or type of e-mail attachments;
■ specify clearly any restrictions on web material that can be viewed or copied. A simple ban on 'offensive material' is unlikely to be clear enough for workers to know what is and is not allowed. Employers should at least give examples of the sort of material that is considered offensive, eg material containing racist terminology or images of nudity;
■ lay down clear rules regarding personal use of communication equipment when used from home;
■ explain the purposes of any monitoring, its extent, and the means used;
■ outline how the policy is enforced and the penalties for breaching it.

Your right to privacy

The best way to conduct any personal e-mail communications at work is to use a private e-mail address, rather than your work one, if your employer's policy allows this. Remember that no e-mail is ever totally secure. The only way to guarantee that you are safely using e-mail or the web at work for personal purposes is to know that you are doing it within your rights for that workplace.

Your employer is entitled to access your in-box or voicemail while you are away from work if he or she believes that there will be business communications that need to be dealt with in your absence and if you have been told that this will happen. The employer should, however, take all possible steps to avoid accessing communications that are clearly not relating to business – we would recommend starting personal e-mail subject lines with 'personal', and do not assume privacy.

Bear in mind though that this will not guarantee any level of privacy if the employer has another reason to intercept your e-mail (for example, if the employer suspects criminal activity, or needs to check that the business is complying with legal obligations).

Vehicle monitoring

Technology increasingly allows employers to monitor vehicles used by workers off-site, such as company cars or delivery vehicles. Devices can record or transmit the location of the vehicle, the distance it has covered, or information about the user's driving habits.

Monitoring vehicle movements where the vehicle is allocated to a specific driver and information about the performance of the vehicle that can be linked to that driver is allowed but regulated by the Data Protection Act. Where private use of the vehicle is allowed, monitoring movements when used privately, without the freely given consent of the user, is rarely justifiable.

In some circumstances, though, employers are actually under a legal obligation to monitor use of vehicles, even when used privately, eg where a tachograph is fitted to a lorry. In this case the legal obligation takes precedence.

The Human Rights Act

The Human Rights Act gives you additional protection at work, but can only be used as part of a complaint under employment or discrimination law. It also gives you general rights as a citizen. As this law is still relatively new, and the rights it contains (drawn from the European Convention on Human Rights) are expressed in general terms, it is hard to know precisely how the courts will interpret it. However, the likely implications of the Act in the workplace flow from its rights to privacy, association and freedom of expression. The data protection rules referred to above have had to take account of the right to privacy. Interception of telephone calls for some limited reasons is generally only allowed under the Interception of Communications Regulations 2000 if potential users of the phone system have been informed that they might be intercepted. This would not stop your employer from checking what calls you had made but they could not listen in on them.

The Human Rights Act further underpins the right to join a trade union and take part in trade union activities. It gives you the right of freedom of expression (subject to defamation laws and the provisions of the Race Relations Act). It also strengthens the right to a fair hearing in a court or tribunal.

Your rights timetable and how to use it

This is where we list all your most important statutory rights at work, how long you have to wait to be entitled to them (the qualifying period), how quickly you must make a formal application (the time limit) and the maximum compensation you can win (although actual awards are often much lower). These compensation limits are usually uprated for inflation each year. The list starts with those that protect you when you apply for a job and finishes with those for which you have to wait the longest.

Table 1.1   Your rights timetable

From when you apply for a job			
Your complaint:	I've been discriminated against on grounds of race, sex, disability or trade union membership.		
Time period:	Three months.	*Maximum compensation:*	Unlimited.
More information in Chapter 6.			

From your first day at work			
Your complaint:	I've not been paid because my employer is insolvent or bankrupt.		
Time period:	Three months from date on which bankruptcy declared.	*Maximum compensation:*	The smaller of £310 or a week's pay.
More information on page 173.			

Your complaint:	There's been an unlawful deduction from my wages.		
Time period:	None while in employment; within three months if employment terminates.	*Maximum compensation:*	The tribunal can order the employer to make up the difference, backdating it to when the deduction started.
More information on page 44.			

Your complaint:	I have been dismissed or discriminated against because:
	■ I've raised a health and safety problem.
	■ I've become pregnant.
	■ I'm a trade union member or pension-fund representative.
	■ I've demanded to be paid the national minimum wage, insisted on my working time rights or taken other action against my employer.
	■ I've taken reasonable time off for study or training, public duties or antenatal care.
	■ I'm a shop worker or similar who has refused to work Sundays.
	■ I blew the whistle on wrongdoings by my employer.
	■ I complained about non-payment of Working Families Tax Credit.

Time period:	Three months starting with date of (last) act or failure to act.	*Maximum compensation:*	Some of these rights have minimum compensation rates, eg, for health and safety dismissals the minimum is £4,200; some have maximum rates and others, for example, whistle-blowing, have no maximum. In some cases the tribunal can order the employer to make good, for example, to pay you the minimum wage.
More information in Chapter 7.			

Your complaint:	I've not been given an itemized pay statement.		
Time period:	None while in employment; within three months if employment terminates.	*Maximum compensation:*	The tribunal can order the employer to provide an itemized pay statement.
More information in Chapter 2.			

Your complaint:	I'm not being paid the minimum wage.		
Time period:	None while in employment, within three months after leaving a job.	*Maximum compensation:*	The tribunal can order the employer to pay the difference between what you were paid and the minimum wage.
More information on page 55.			

Your complaint:	I've not been allowed to see the records I need to see to make sure I am getting the minimum wage.		
Time period:	Three months after the fourteenth day following receipt of production notice unless a later date agreed.	Maximum compensation:	Tribunal can order access and/or compensation of up to 80 times the current hourly minimum wage.
More information on page 55.			

Your complaint:	I've been dismissed or treated unfairly because I've 'asserted a statutory right', ie taken a case against my employer such as claiming unlawful deduction from wages.		
Time period:	Three months starting with date of dismissal or detriment.	Maximum compensation:	If dismissed, basic award up to £310 per week's pay lost, to a limit of £9,300 plus up to £60,600 compensatory award. If still working, the tribunal can order compensation and order the employer to stop the unfair treatment. No maximum.
More information in Chapter 7.			

Your complaint:	I've been dismissed or treated unfairly because I made complaints about health and safety, or for whistle-blowing.		
Time period:	Three months starting with date of dismissal or detriment.	Maximum compensation:	If dismissed, basic award up to £310 per week's pay lost, to a limit of £9,300. No maximum compensatory award.
As from 1 February 2007. These figures increase each year.			

Your complaint:	My employer has breached my contract.		
Time period:	Three months and only after termination at an employment tribunal; six years after the breach occurred in the courts.	*Maximum compensation:*	Maximum in tribunals of £25,000. Limit of £50,000 in lower (county or sheriff's courts), unlimited in higher courts.
More information on page 123.			

Your complaint:	I've been sacked because of my sex, race or disability.		
Time period:	Three months starting with effective date of termination.	*Maximum compensation:*	Unlimited.
More information in Chapter 6.			

Your complaint:	I'm not getting the proper rest breaks set out in the working time rules.		
Time period:	Three months starting on the day on which the failure occurred.	*Maximum compensation:*	Unlimited and/or the tribunal can order the employer to provide proper rest breaks for you.
More information in Chapter 3.			

Your complaint:	I'm getting paid less than people doing similar jobs because of my sex.		
Time period:	Six months starting with date of act complained of, or from date employment ended.	Maximum compensation:	Tribunal can order employer to provide equal pay and/or order compensation.

More information in Chapter 6.

One month from the start of your job

Your complaint:	I've been laid off but not paid (guarantee pay).		
Time period:	Three months starting with day for which payment claimed.	Maximum compensation:	£19.60 per day.

More information on page 23.

Your complaint:	I have been suspended on medical grounds.		
Time period:	Three months starting with effective date of suspension.	Maximum compensation:	The pay you have lost.

More information on page 24.

Two months from the start of your job

Your complaint:	I've not been given a written statement of employment particulars.		
Time period:	None while in employment; within three months if employment terminates.	Maximum compensation:	The tribunal can order the employer to provide a written statement; the tribunal should award minimum compensation of £620.

More information on page 19.

After 13 weeks employment			
Your complaint:	I'm not getting paid holidays.		
Time period:	Three months from the date when the leave should have been permitted to begin.	*Maximum compensation:*	Unlimited and/or the tribunal can order the employer to give you your leave entitlement.
More information in Chapter 3.			

After a year in your job			
Your complaint:	I've been dismissed unfairly.		
Time period:	Three calendar months from when you were dismissed.	*Maximum compensation:*	Basic award up to £310 per week's pay lost, to a limit of £9,300, plus up to £60,600 compensatory award.
More information in Chapter 7.			

Your complaint:	I've been dismissed because the owners of my business have changed.		
Time period:	Three months starting with the effective date of termination.	*Maximum compensation:*	Basic award up to £310 per week's pay lost, to a limit of £9,300, plus up to £60,600 compensatory award.
More information on page 22.			

Your complaint:	I've not been given written reasons for dismissal.		
Time period:	Three months starting with effective date of termination.	*Maximum compensation:*	Two weeks' pay.
More information in Chapter 7.			

Your complaint:	I've not been allowed to return to work after additional maternity leave.		
Time period:	Three months after notified day of return when employer refuses right.	Maximum compensation:	Unlimited.
More information on page 83.			

Your complaint:	I have not been allowed to take parental leave or time off for a family emergency under the terms of the regulations.		
Time period:	Three months.	Maximum compensation:	Unlimited.
More information on page 95 and page 105.			

After two years			
Your complaint:	I've not been paid my redundancy pay.		
Time period:	Six months starting from the date of dismissal.	Maximum compensation:	See Chapter 7.
More information on page 169.			

All the figures given for compensation are correct for 2007–08. Most are uprated, often by inflation, each year. They may therefore have increased by the time you read this.

2

Payday

It is good to have a satisfying and worthwhile job, but most of us work because we need the money as well. This chapter sets out the law about your pay – what your employer must tell you, what he or she can deduct from your pay and the minimum he or she must pay you.

Deductions from wages

Your contract of employment or 'written statement of employment particulars' will say how much you are going to be paid. It must be at least the minimum wage, described later in this chapter. If you do not receive the pay promised in your contract or written statement then your employer has made an 'unauthorized deduction from wages' and you can take a claim to an Employment Tribunal (see Chapter 8). This statutory right covers all workers, not just employees (see page 9 for this important distinction).

There are, however, three ways in which it is legal for your employer to take money from your wage or salary:

■ Your employer can deduct income tax and National Insurance. This must be for the correct amount. If you think it is not, contact HM Revenue & Customs and it will repay you if the amount deducted was wrong, or investigate your employer if there is a suspicion of fraud.

▪ Your employer can take money if you have given permission. For example, you may agree to make a payroll contribution to a charity, or to a staff social club or to a trade union. You can however withdraw your permission at any time.

▪ Your employer can make a deduction from your wage packet if your contract allows this to happen, as long as you have seen the contract with this in it before you start work, or your employer has explained in writing to you that they intend to take the money and you have agreed to it. This then becomes part of your contract.

If your employer has overpaid you the previous time you were paid, they may take that from your next pay packet without asking you. If your contract allows your employer to take money away as part of a disciplinary process, they can do this without asking you (see Chapter 5). If you take part in a strike, your employer can take money from your wages without asking you. In this situation, your union may give you strike pay.

There are some jobs that allow your employer to deduct money if there is a cash shortage due to theft. The key test is whether you deal with the public and handle money. So if you are a shop worker, or your job involves selling goods to the public, you can have money deducted from your wages if there is a shortfall. This can also happen if you collect money, say as a rent collector. But it does not apply if you only deal in business to business transactions, perhaps as a lorry driver supplying goods to a warehouse.

Your employer cannot deduct more than 10 per cent of your cheque, salary or wages packet. They can keep on making a 10 per cent deduction until the loss is paid off. The 10 per cent is before tax or National Insurance is deducted. Depending on your tax situation this may mean that in practice more or less than 10 per cent of your take home pay may be deducted. However, if you are leaving your job, whether because you have resigned, retired or been dismissed, your employer can deduct any amount of your final pay packet and any notice pay (see Chapter 7) to make up the shortfall.

Your employer must start making any deductions from your wages within 12 months of the loss occurring. But while they cannot start deductions after 12 months, they can continue if they have already started before the 12-month limit. A new deduction, however, would be unlawful and you can take a tribunal case.

The law on 'unauthorized deductions' covers issues such as holiday pay, bonuses, Statutory Sick Pay and luncheon vouchers. It does not cover loans or advances of wages, pensions or redundancy payments, tips, or payments in kind.

If you think that your employer has wrongly deducted money from your wages you should raise the matter with them first, or with the finance department if you work for a large company. It may be that a genuine mistake was made. If this is not the case, you can make a complaint to an Employment Tribunal (see Chapter 8) and they can order the employer to pay the money.

Sick pay rights

When they talk about their sick pay most workers mean the scheme operated by their employers. There are no national rules for these schemes, and many exclude some people, such as new staff.

But you do have rights to Statutory Sick Pay, a flat-rate benefit, paid by your employer, in accordance with national rules. It is often called SSP for short. If you are covered, your employer must either pay you Statutory Sick Pay when you qualify; or open up the company scheme to you, and offer you benefits that are at least as good.

This is a complicated subject and this section has to simplify some points. If you have any problems claiming Statutory Sick Pay, make sure you get advice and support from your union or an advice agency as soon as possible.

Qualifying for sick pay

You will qualify for Statutory Sick Pay if you:

▦ are an employee – see page 9 for the difference between an employee and a worker. As long as you are an employee it does not matter whether you work part-time or have only just started work with an employer;
▦ were over 16 and under 65 when your sickness began;
▦ earn enough to pay National Insurance Contributions (£90 a week from April 2008).

You don't have to have actually paid any Contributions; earning above that level is enough to qualify. If your pay fluctuates, then entitlement depends on your average pay over the last eight weeks.

You will *not* qualify if you:

▦ are self-employed;
▦ have not started work yet;
▦ have a contract of employment that lasts less than three months – but people who have actually been employed for more than three months will usually qualify, even if their original contract was for less than that.

Claiming Statutory Sick Pay

▦ SSP is normally paid in the same way as your wages, and you claim it on a form from your employer.
▦ You can get it for up to 28 weeks if your sickness lasts that long.
▦ You will not be paid for the first three days – these are called 'waiting days'.
▦ Two periods of sickness within 56 days are treated as linked. This means that you won't face waiting days for the second. On the other hand, time off in the first will count towards the 28-week limit;

■ You are not entitled to SSP once your contract of employment ends.

■ Nor once your Maternity Allowance or Statutory
Maternity Pay period begins, or, if you are not entitled to
either of these for a pregnancy-related reason, in the six
weeks before your baby is due.

■ Employers can ask for 'reasonable evidence' of incapacity.
In practice, this means a self-certification form for the first
seven days (including the waiting days) and a doctor's
certificate after that.

■ If your employer dismisses you to avoid paying SSP you
may have a claim for unfair dismissal at an Employment
Tribunal. The SSP rules, in any case, require them to go on
paying you the SSP until you are no longer entitled to the
benefit (or your contract comes to an end, if this is earlier).

■ If there is a stoppage of work due to a trade dispute that
began *before* you became sick, you will not be entitled to
SSP for the whole period of incapacity, even if the dispute
ends. On the other hand, if the stoppage began *after* you
became sick, you will continue to be entitled to SSP.

How much will you get?

Statutory Sick Pay is paid at a flat rate of £72.55 a week.
Normally it is uprated each April. If you have two or more
jobs, and earn more than enough to pay National Insurance
Contributions in both, you can claim SSP in each.

Sick of the sack

Joyce Khan was a night-duty nurse, but became ill and was off
sick for some time. Under NHS rules (part of her contract of
employment) she was entitled to sick pay of two months' full
pay and two months' half pay. But when this four-month period
came to an end, Joyce was sacked.

However, the booklet setting out NHS sick pay provisions said nothing about dismissal at the end of the sick pay period. Her managers said that such a rule existed nationally in the Health Service and that it had been applied to other cases. But Joyce had, in fact, already sent in a medical certificate indicating that within 10 days of her sick pay running out she expected to be back on duty. Apparently this certificate had never reached the attention of the officer who dealt with the dismissal.

She claimed unfair dismissal and won. The tribunal said that Joyce's managers had not acted reasonably. A rule that dismissal should be automatic on termination of sick pay, regardless of individual circumstances, was outmoded. Secondly, there had been bad communication between departments concerning the medical certificate, and thirdly there had been no consultation with the employee concerned before dismissal.

Tribunal cases have established what an employer should do before dismissal for sickness, and there is guidance in the ACAS Code on Discipline. Employers should: consult the employee and discuss the problem with him or her; take steps to enable him or her to take a balanced view of the problem (this will include taking steps to ascertain the medical situation); consider whether suitable alternative work is available.

It is possible for an employer to fairly dismiss a worker for genuine sickness by reason of capability. But tribunals tend to look carefully at the reasonableness in such cases. They will consider the length of past and future service of the employee; how vital the employee is to the employer's business, and how easy it is to find a temporary replacement; the effect of the absence on the business and other employees.

The question a tribunal will ask is whether the time has come where a reasonable employer is entitled to say enough is enough. The key is then likely to be the future sickness of the worker. But the employer must also ensure that they are not breaking the Disability Discrimination Act (see Chapter 6).

The national mininimum wage

The vast majority of workers and employees are entitled to the national minimum wage (or the NMW as we will call it in the rest of this chapter). You are covered whether or not you have a written contract of employment. Home workers, agency workers and piece and commission workers are all entitled to the NMW. So are workers on temporary contracts and part-time workers. However 'casual' the work, you are still entitled to be paid the NMW. Agricultural workers are covered by a different set of minimum wages, depending on age and qualification (rates are available from the Agricultural Helpline: 0845 00 00 134).

The following groups are *not* entitled to the NMW:

■ family workers, including those working for a family business.

■ people working within a family, sharing tasks and leisure activities, for example au pairs;

■ trainees on government-funded schemes, in particular New Deal participants who are on either the Voluntary or Environmental Task Force options;

■ apprentices aged up to 18 and older apprentices in the first year of their apprenticeship;

■ students on work placements, including teacher-training placements.

■ the armed forces;

■ prisoners;

■ share fishermen;

■ mariners and offshore workers based entirely outside the UK;

■ voluntary workers (who must work for a charity, voluntary organization, school or hospital and must not receive any payments other than reasonable expenses or benefits in kind or, in certain circumstances, subsistence payments). Some people who are considered volunteers may actually be workers who should be paid the NMW because they have what amounts to a contractual relationship. These include some internships that have not been arranged as an integral part of an educational course.

In some sectors where there are many more people who would like a job than there are vacancies, such as politics, the media and entertainment, some employers demand a period of free work variously described as a placement, work experience or other euphemism before considering someone for a paid job. This is a racket and is likely to be in breach of the NMW.

Work experience can of course be educational, and there is a fine line to be drawn here. If the experience is arranged by a school or college then there is probably no legal problem. If it is implicitly or explicitly a try-out period to see if an employer wants to give you a job then there is almost certainly a breach of the law. A good source of advice is the National Council for Work Experience.

The treatment of the self-employed can be complicated. As we saw in the Introduction it is possible to be a worker without being an employee. Both employees and workers are, however, covered by the NMW. If you have a contract for services rather than a contract of employment then you are still entitled to the minimum wage. If, however, you are genuinely self-employed, effectively running your own business and cannot be said to have an employer, then you are not covered by the NMW. Your tax status is once again not a guide to your minimum wage status. You can be treated as self-employed by the tax office, but still be eligible for the minimum wage. If in doubt, take advice.

National minimum wage hourly rates

You are entitled to be paid the NMW for each hour you work. But young workers are entitled to a lower rate than older workers, as are some workers receiving training. Hourly rates are currently:

adult workers aged 22 and over	£5.52
18- to 21-year-olds (the Youth Development rate)	£4.60
16- to 17-year-olds above the school leaving age	£3.40

These rates apply up to October 2008. They usually increase each year in October.

Calculating your hourly pay

Hourly pay for the national minimum wage is worked out as an average over your pay period. If you are paid weekly, your pay period is a week. If you are paid daily, it is a day, and if monthly, it is a month. Some people are paid in arrears. For example, your pay for the work you do one week may be actually paid in the next week.

Working out your hourly pay for most people is a simple matter of dividing your total pay (before tax and other deductions) by the number of hours you worked. But there can be complications, and there are rules about both what does and does not count as pay and how your hours of work are counted.

What counts as pay

Your pay may be made up of a mix of different elements. The following *do* count towards your hourly rate:

■ gross pay – before national insurance, tax or pension deductions;
■ piece rates, sales commissions, any performance-related pay;
■ a bonus (though it must be allocated mainly to the pay period in which it is paid);
■ tips paid through the payroll, though tips paid in cash directly to staff are in addition to your hourly rate.

The following do *not* count:

■ pension, retirement or redundancy payments;
■ overtime and shift payments;
■ expenses or money spent on work refunded by the employer;
■ allowances such as London Weighting;
■ loans or advance of wages;
■ any benefits in kind, such as meals, luncheon vouchers, car allowance or medical insurance, except accommodation which is dealt with below.

This means that any payments for overtime, for example, or London Weighting, must be in addition to an average hourly rate of at least the NMW. Your employer cannot pay you £3 an hour for an eight-hour day and then £6 an hour for an extra four hours overtime, and claim that on average you were getting more than the minimum wage. Overtime payments cannot be used to boost a basic average that is below the NMW. Nor can an employer add a notional amount to your pay to take it to the minimum wage level but then deduct it again to pay for any meals or drinks provided free.

If accommodation is provided as part of your job, your employer can deduct a maximum of £4.30 for every day accommodation is provided. This means that a maximum of £30.10 per week can be deducted for accommodation from your pay.

The accommodation charge is the only deduction that an employer can make from the minimum wage for non-pay benefits. Your employer may not charge for travel, meals, uniforms or services like gas, water and electricity if to do so would take your pay below the minimum wage. Employers cannot charge for protective clothing or other necessary health and safety equipment in any circumstances. The law also stops employers from getting round these restrictions by splitting their business into separate employment and accommodation agencies.

What count as working hours

Hourly paid and salaried workers are entitled to be paid the NMW for time:

- at work and required to be at work;
- on standby or on-call at or near work;
- downtime at work caused by machine breakdown;
- travelling to business or training during normal working hours;
- training during normal working hours.

If you are hourly paid, the NMW legislation does not give you the right to be paid for rest breaks, sick leave or maternity leave. However, under your employment contract you may be entitled to be paid for these hours too.

Output

Some workers have no set hours but are paid only for the output they produce. Most home workers engaged in manufacturing or envelope-stuffing jobs are paid in this way, as are many newspaper and leaflet distributors and travelling sales-people.

If you have set hours and are paid by results then you are not an output worker but a time worker and should simply be paid the minimum wage. Employers can also choose to pay the minimum wage for each hour worked to genuine output workers as well. There are however some special provisions for output workers because employers often have no way of checking how many hours such workers have actually worked.

Employers are allowed to use what is called the 'fair piece rates' system. This requires them to establish how long it takes an average worker to do the job. They should do this by timing a fair sample of workers to get an average time and then adding 20 per cent to allow for fatigue during the day.

Unmeasured work

A small number of workers undertake 'unmeasured work'. This means they have fixed tasks, but no fixed hours of work. Examples might include hostel wardens or domestic workers with no fixed hours. Workers undertaking unmeasured work must either be paid at least the NMW for every hour worked, or can agree a 'daily average' agreement with their employer. This would identify the number of hours likely to be worked daily, and must be a realistic average. The worker must then be paid at least the NMW for this number of hours each day.

Your right to see your records

Employers are required to keep sufficient records to establish that they are paying workers at least the NMW and workers have the right to see and copy their records. If you want to see your records, you must ask your employer in writing. The employer must produce the records within 14 days. You have the right to be accompanied by someone of your choice when you inspect your records.

What to do if you are not receiving the NMW

Your rights

Under the NMW legislation, you have the right:

- to be paid at least NMW rates;
- to see your records (accompanied) as set out above;
- not to be dismissed or victimized as a result of attempts to be paid or ensure you are eligible for the NMW.

If you are not receiving the NMW, or have been refused access to your records or have been victimized as a result of trying to claim the NMW, you can get help to enforce your rights.

Take advice

If you are a trade union member, your union will be able to give you advice on your rights, accompany you to see your records and help you take a case to an Employment Tribunal if you are not receiving your rights. Other agencies including Low Pay Units around the country can also help and advise. Their numbers are given at the end of the book.

National helpline and enforcement officers

HM Revenue & Customs (HMRC) is responsible for enforcing the NMW. It runs a national helpline, which gives information and advice on the NMW. Enforcement officers at the Inland Revenue can help you to work out whether you are receiving your rights, and take enforcement action against your employer if you are not. Calls are charged at local rates, and are confidential.

Enforcement officers have legal powers to enable them to enforce the NMW. They can require your employer to provide information about NMW pay, and inspect your employer's premises to gain access to pay records. If an enforcement officer believes that an employer is not paying the NMW, he or she can serve an enforcement notice that requires your employer to start paying you the NMW and pay you back pay.

If an employer ignores the enforcement notice, the enforcement officer can serve a fixed penalty notice of £224.70 for each underpaid worker. These fines, though, go to the government, not to you. The enforcement officers can also help workers take their employer to an Employment Tribunal, or take a case on behalf of the worker. HMRC can also pursue claims for ex-workers who have left the offending employer. This matters, because most workers actually make their complaint after they have resigned. HMRC have so far recovered £23 million for underpaid workers.

Deliberate refusal to pay the NMW is a criminal offence. If an employer continues to refuse payment, the enforcement officer can prosecute them in the criminal courts.

Employment tribunal or civil courts

You can take a case against your employer in an employment tribunal or in the civil courts to recover any money owed as a result of not receiving the NMW. It is up to the employer to show that they have paid you the NMW. You do not have to prove that you have not received it, though in practice you will need to be able to disprove your employer's claim.

You are, however, probably best advised to make every effort to get HMRC 's enforcement officers to take up your case if possible, especially if it is a clear-cut case. Tribunals are more likely to hear test cases, where the rules are not entirely clear. For example, sub-post office masters and mistresses have established that they are workers and therefore entitled to the NMW through tribunal cases.

If you have been refused access to your records, an employment tribunal can order your employer to pay you £441.60 (80 times the national rate). You can also take a claim to an Employment Tribunal for unfair dismissal or victimization if you have lost your job or suffered some other action from your employer resulting from trying to get your right to be paid the NMW.

Tax credits

Tax credits are the government's chosen way of providing extra incomes to parents and low-paid workers. They are notoriously complicated, and this guide does not have the space to explain all the rules – if you have more detailed questions a good place to start is the tax credit helpline: 0845 300 3900.

There are two tax credits:

■ Child Tax Credit (CTC) supports families with children, regardless of whether anyone in the family has a paid job.
■ Working Tax Credit (WTC) helps low-paid workers (including some workers without children) by topping up their earnings.

Rules that apply to both CTC and WTC

There are some general rules about who can get CTC and WTC:

▦ You must be at least 16 years old.
▦ Normally, you must live in the UK.
▦ You must not be subject to immigration control.
▦ If you are a member of a couple (married, civil partners or living with someone as if you are married or civil partners), you must claim together, as the circumstances of both will be taken into account.

Child Tax Credit

CTC helps families with children, whether or not you are in employment. To qualify, you must be responsible for at least one child or young person:

▦ a child (people are counted as children until 1 September after their sixteenth birthday); *or*
▦ a young person aged 16 to 19 and in full-time education or unwaged training; *or*
▦ a young person aged 16 or 17 who has registered with the Careers Service/Connexions.

CTC is paid direct to the person with main responsibility for caring for the children (if you also qualify for the childcare element of WTC, you will be paid this at the same time). CTC is made up of two parts:

▦ The *family element*, for every family with children. There is a higher rate (known as the *baby element*) if you have a child under the age of one.
▦ A *child element* for each child, paid at a higher rate for disabled children and an enhanced rate for severely disabled children.

CTC is designed to give the most support to families who need it most. The amount you get depends on your family's income, but families with incomes of up to just over £58,000 a year qualify for some CTC.

Working Tax Credit

WTC tops up the incomes of people with low incomes who are employed or self-employed, including some people who do not have children. It provides extra support for disabled people and helps with childcare costs.

You can qualify for WTC if you are aged over 25 and work for at least 30 hours a week. There are also ways to qualify if you are aged over 16 and work over 16 hours a week:

■ if you are responsible for a child or young person;
■ if you are disabled: you must have a disability that puts you at a disadvantage in getting a job and receive a qualifying benefit;
■ if you are aged over 50 and returning to paid work after being on out-of-work benefits.

WTC is no longer paid via your employer; it is now paid direct to your bank or building society. If you and your partner are both working 16 hours or more a week, you will have to choose who it is paid to.

WTC is made up of a series of elements:

■ a basic element;
■ an element for lone parents and couples;
■ an element for working a total of at least 30 hours a week (only one element per couple);
■ a disability element;
■ a severe disability element;
■ an element if you are aged at least 50 and returning to employment – this is paid at a higher rate if you are returning to employment of at least 30 hours a week;
■ a childcare element – see below.

Like CTC, the WTC is designed to provide the most help to the people who need it most, and the amount you will actually get depends on how high your income is from other sources. You can have an income of nearly £15,000 a year and still qualify for some WTC.

Help with childcare

WTC can also help with the costs of childcare – this is known as the 'childcare element'. To qualify, you must be:

- a lone parent employed for at least 16 hours a week; *or*
- a member of a couple where both partners work at least 16 hours a week; *or*
- a member of a couple where one partner works 16 hours a week and the other is incapacitated.

The childcare element pays for up to 80 per cent of the costs of registered or approved childcare, up to a limit of £175 a week for one child or £300 for two or more.

Your childcare element is added to the other WTC elements you qualify for, and the total amount you get will depend on your income (joint income for couples) but it will not necessarily be paid in the same way. If you qualify for the childcare element, this is always paid direct to the person with main responsibility for caring for the children, alongside the CTC, even if he or she is not the person who receives the WTC.

Extra help

You can check whether you qualify for tax credits online at http://www.taxcredits.inlandrevenue.gov.uk, and the website also provides extra information about tax credits.

There is a tax credits helpdesk, which can help you make a claim or report changes in your circumstances, open from 8 am to 8 pm seven days a week: 0845 300 3900 (textphone: 0845 300 3909; Welsh helpline: 0845 302 1489).

3

Working time rights

Thanks to Europe's working time directive, most people now have seven basic rights to proper time off, rest breaks and paid holiday:

- four weeks' paid holiday a year;
- a break when the working day is more than six hours;
- a rest period of 11 hours every working day;
- a rest period of 24 hours once every seven days;
- a ceiling of 48 hours on the maximum average working week;
- a ceiling of an average of 8 hours' night work in every 24;
- free health assessment for night workers.

But working time rights are complicated, have proved controversial and are barely enforced. Employer organizations successfully lobbied our government for exemptions and opt-outs that do not apply in the rest of Europe. The European regulations, on which UK law is based, are far from comprehensive. There are many problems of definition such as what exactly counts as working time. Many provisions can be varied by agreement between the employer and the workforce.

We work longer hours than any other European country; more than 3 million of us work more than 48 hours per week. In some industries and sectors this is because many hours of overtime are worked. Security guards working for the minimum wage need the overtime to earn a decent income. In other sectors long hours are built into the system, with junior hospital doctors probably the best-known example.

For white-collar workers the basic problem is unpaid overtime. The biggest growth in working hours in recent years has been among managers, professionals and those doing similar jobs. It is rare for employees doing these types of job to have their hours counted, as they will not normally get overtime pay. But many offices and other workplaces are still gripped by a long-hours culture. Nothing is ever said directly but the sheer volume of work, pressure from colleagues, job insecurity and wanting to get on have all conspired to keep people at work for longer and longer hours.

Many such jobs are rewarding and interesting. Work does not always come along in neat nine to five parcels. But it is easy for working hours to ratchet up a little more each year. Work and family life get out of balance. Stress and exhaustion levels rise. To call time on Britain's long-hours culture is not to go back to clockwatching, but to understand that other countries manage to combine better living standards, shorter working hours and more productive workplaces.

Then of course there are those who are missing out on their most basic rights to paid holidays and proper rest breaks. When the Working Time Regulations (WTR) first came into force in 1998, around 2 million people won their first ever rights to paid holidays. Some are still missing out, or are being made to pay in other ways for their own holidays.

This chapter aims to guide you through the working time maze. It cannot provide all the answers but it should tell you whether you are getting your working time rights, whether you are clearly missing out, or whether you are in a grey area where you will need to take detailed advice based on your own circumstances.

Exemptions from Working Time Regulations

Some groups of workers are covered by their own special rules. Others miss out on some rights but not others. If you are under 18 the rules are different, and you should make sure you read the section on pages 78–79 at the end of this chapter. The following groups are covered:

■ **Transport workers** were originally exempt from the WTR but 'non-mobile' transport workers such as station staff have been fully covered since 2003, while 'mobile' rail staff such as drivers and guards as well as non-HGV/PSV drivers of road vehicles are partly covered. These workers are entitled to an average maximum working week of 48 hours; however, they are only entitled to 'adequate' rest, rather than the stronger rights to breaks and rest periods that apply to most workers. There is no definition of 'adequate', but the TUC believes that it needs to be as good as 'compensatory' rest (see below). Staff who work at a transport location such as people who unload lorries or who work in shops in stations are covered by the working time rules.

■ **HGV and PSV drivers** get four weeks' paid leave. They are also covered by the rules in the Road Transport Working Time Regulations, which limit their hours to 48 a week without any opt-out. However, many employers try to misuse the loophole that allows waiting time known about in advance not to count against the 48-hour week.

■ **Seafarers** are covered by separate rules.

■ **Aviation and cabin crew** have their own rules too.

■ **Junior doctors in training** will be covered by the 48-hour limit from 2009.

■ **Armed forces and civil protection services** (such as the police – but not all civil protection personnel) are excluded. Ambulance personnel, fire-fighters and prison staff are covered by the regulations. You will need to take more advice if you work in this category. Most workers in civil protection outside the armed forces or the police are in a trade union. This should be your first port of call for further advice.

■ **Domestic staff in a private household** are partially excluded. They are entitled to rest breaks and paid holidays, but not to the 48-hour average week or night work rights.

■ **Those whose 'working time is not measured or pre-determined'** – although workers in this category are entitled to paid holidays, they are exempt from all other working time rights.

This last exemption has been the subject of much argument in Britain. The European regulations are clear that this is meant to be a narrow exclusion aimed at relatively small groups in the workforce. These include top managers who are free to set their own hours (perhaps because they own the business or have no one to tell them what to do), workers employed by other members of their family and some unusual jobs such as ministers of religion.

Employer organizations have argued that this exemption should apply to the majority of white-collar workers, for work they do on a 'voluntary' basis outside the hours set down in their contract of employment, but the European Court of Justice has ruled against this broad interpretation. We explain this later in the chapter.

Happy holidays!

Everyone at work is entitled to a minimum of 4.8 weeks' paid leave each year. The number of days you will actually receive as holiday depends on how many days a week you work. If you work full-time five days a week you should, therefore, get 4.8 lots of five days – that's 24 days – of paid leave every year.

If you work part-time you should get 4.8 times what you work on average each week. For example, if you work three days a week then you should get (4.8 × 3 =) 14.4 days' holiday.

The entitlement will increase to 5.6 weeks of leave from 1 April 2009. But this is not in addition to bank holidays. Christmas Day and other holidays can count as part of your annual entitlement as long as you are paid for them. However, the European minimum is only four weeks. The UK was the only EU country that allowed public holidays to count against this minimum. A long union campaign led the government to deal with this by extending the four-week minimum by eight days for full-time workers in two stages – first to 4.8, and then to 5.6 weeks in 2009, as there are eight bank holidays in Britain. There are more details about transitional arrangements on the worksMART website run by the TUC at www.worksmart.org.uk. You can also take unpaid time off if you have young children or suffer a family emergency such as looking after a sick child. This is explained in Chapter 4.

When you can take your holidays

You do not have the right to choose when you take your holiday. This is almost entirely up to your employer. Unless your contract says otherwise, they can refuse requests, rule out all holiday at particular times of the year and even direct you to take your holiday when it suits them without any consultation with you. If you are requesting a holiday, the regulations say that you must give your employer sufficient notice. This is twice the number of days of leave that will be taken – to take four days off work you must therefore give eight working days' notice.

But while you must give this notice, it does not guarantee that you will get the holiday, as your employer is free to refuse leave requests. On the other hand, there is nothing to stop your employer granting requests at extremely short notice for that matter. In practice, most well-run organizations will have their own rules about deciding leave.

More importantly, the same notice period applies to your employer if they are telling you when you must take a holiday. They cannot therefore force you to take a fortnight's leave because an order is suddenly cancelled. They must give you four weeks' notice – twice the period of the leave – if they are to make you take two weeks off.

Your employer must also give you notice if they want to rule out some periods when staff cannot take leave. The period of notice must be the same as the period during which holiday cannot be taken. In other words, if the employer wants to stop people taking holidays for the four-week period before Christmas, then four weeks' notice must be given.

Holiday pay

If you work regular hours and get the same pay each week, then holiday pay is simply the same as your normal pay. If your normal pay includes regular bonuses, shift premiums or contractual overtime payments then these should also be included in your holiday pay – voluntary overtime does not count.

If your weekly pay varies because your hours vary from week to week, then your weekly holiday pay should be the average weekly pay you earned over the last 12 weeks. This should include statutory overtime, shift pay and any bonuses.

Holiday pay paid throughout the year

When paid holidays were first introduced in 1998, some people found a change to their pay slip. Their take home pay was still the same, but it was now made up of two elements. First was their basic pay, which had been reduced from what it had been in previous pay packets. The difference was made up with a second new element called holiday pay. The employer then said that there was no need for paid holidays as you were getting your holiday pay through the year and it was up to you to save it up. However, a European Court of Justice case brought by a union in 2006 has made this illegal.

Changing jobs and holiday rights

You cannot take unused holiday from one job to another. When you leave a job you should get holiday pay for any unused holiday and may have to pay some holiday pay back if you have taken more holiday than you are entitled to.

The amount is worked out using what is called your 'leave year'. This is the period during which you can take your four weeks' leave. Most workers will have a leave year defined as part of their contract of employment or in a staff handbook, and will be the same across the organization. Contractual leave years usually start in April or January. If no leave year is defined in this way then your leave year runs between each anniversary of when you started your job.

The amount of holiday you are entitled to for part of a leave year is worked out on an obvious basis. You get one-twelfth of your holiday entitlement for each month you have worked, which is one week's holiday for every three months of your leave year. If you leave after six months and have taken all your four weeks' leave then your employer could make you pay back two weeks' pay. On the other hand, if you have taken no holiday then your employer owes you two weeks' pay.

Days off and breaks

The basic rights are easily stated. You should get at least one day off every week and an uninterrupted break of 11 hours every day.

But it does not have to be the same day each week. As an example, your employer can meet the weekly rest requirement by giving you the first day of one week and the last day of the next. This means you can legally work 12 days in a row without a day off, as long as you then get two days off in a row.

If this were adopted as a regular work pattern it would mean you were getting two days off a fortnight, as the rest period on the last day of the second week would be followed by the rest day of the first week in the pattern.

But some workers and jobs are treated differently. These include:

■ security guards, caretakers and other jobs where you need to be there to protect people and property;
■ where the job involves long travelling distances;
■ where the job requires continuity of service or production such as hospitals, prisons, docks, airports, media, post and telecommunications, civil protection (such as the police), agriculture, and industries where work cannot be interrupted (eg, utilities);
■ jobs where there are seasonal rushes such as tourism, post and agriculture;
■ shift workers when they are in the process of changing shift.

The right can also be suspended at any workplace for workers directly involved if there is an emergency or accident. However, if you fall into one of these categories, or are faced with an emergency, you do not lose the right to time off. Instead your employer must provide what the regulations call 'compensatory rest' (see page 70). This must provide the same time off, but at a time convenient to the employer.

Breaks at work

You are also entitled to a break of 20 minutes away from where you normally work if your working day is longer than six hours. But the same groups of workers, who have different provisions for daily and weekly breaks, can also have their breaks at work varied. Again, if you cannot take your break, you must be given 'compensatory rest' or time off at another time (or 'adequate rest' for transport workers).

In some jobs you may be entitled to longer breaks for health and safety reasons. If your job is particularly repetitive or dangerous (keyboard workers liable to RSI are one example) then you may be entitled to more breaks. Take further advice if you are in this position. In a unionized workplace there will normally be a health and safety representative. If not, you can ask the Health and Safety Executive.

Agreeing provisions

Provisions can be varied but only by agreement between the management and the relevant workforce collectively. Your boss cannot call you into his or her office and suggest that you give up or change your breaks, whether it is done politely or with threats of what might happen if you do not. Even through collective agreement you cannot agree to give up your entitlement to breaks, but their timing can be varied.

There are two main ways these agreements can be made. In the regulations these are called collective and workforce agreements. A collective agreement is made between recognized trade unions and management as part of the normal negotiating process. Typically, some sensible flexibility will be agreed in return for some benefit. For example, a different break pattern might be agreed in return for longer breaks. Both sides can benefit from this type of agreement.

A workforce agreement can be made only where there are no recognized unions. The employer will organize an election for work-force representatives who will then conclude an agreement. This is not a very satisfactory procedure. It is very much under the control of the employer. The representatives that are elected are unlikely to be experts on the working time regulations, have any training in how to negotiate or be able to call on expert outside advice. Without union back-up workforce representatives are much less likely to get a good deal.

If this is going on in your workplace, you may want to discuss with an appropriate union how best to use it as a way of unionizing your fellow workers. At the very least you should make sure the elected representatives are genuinely independent of the employer and are as briefed as they can be on what the regulations say.

Some minor provisions can also be varied in your contract of employment.

Working out 'compensatory rest'

Even if you fall into one of the categories, which means you are not covered by some of the rules on breaks, you should still get 'compensatory rest.' This means that you may have to take your breaks or time off at a different time. You can check this by working out how many hours a week in total you are getting as time off, either as breaks at work or between shifts. On average it should be more than 92 hours.

The rules for compensatory rest are not set out in detail, but the government suggests that you should not have to wait more than a couple of weeks for daily rest or more than a couple of months for weekly rest. If you look at your last eight weeks at work and find that you have not had 92 hours' average rest then your employer should be clear about how you can catch up.

The 48-hour working week

The basic right is easily stated – there should be a limit of 48 hours on the maximum average working week. But:

■ some jobs are not covered at all or have different rules;
■ the 48-hour limit is an average – not a limit each week;
■ the average is calculated in different ways for different types of job;
■ individuals and groups of workers can change the way the limit applies or opt out from it altogether.

There are also some real problems defining some of the terms used in the regulations. Many modern (and some older) jobs have grey areas where there is room for argument about whether or not you are actually working.

Defining working time

The basic definition of working time is that you need to be at your workplace and carrying out your working duties under the direction of your employer for it to count as working time. This means that it *does not include*:

■ breaks;
■ travel to work time;
■ time when you are on call but not working;
■ training at a college;
■ time taken to travel to an occasional meeting away from your normal workplace.

It *does include*:

■ overtime;
■ training at the workplace provided by your employer;
■ time taken travelling to visit clients when this is a regular part of your job such as a travelling salesman or home help;
■ a working lunch;
■ being on call at your place of work.

The main arguments about the 48-hour average limit have been about how to define working time for white-collar workers. Some 2.8 million white-collar workers regularly work more than 48 hours per week. The regulations were changed after employer lobbying, but they were then repealed after a union complained to the EU, which said they broke European law.

The problem with these rules is that there is a very fine line between some of the distinctions used. It is rare that white-collar workers are told, 'you will stay in the office until 7 pm'. It is more likely to be the pressure of work and peer group pressure that leads to people working long hours. Employers are likely to claim that all white-collar work outside the hours set in the contract of employment is voluntary.

No one knows how the courts will interpret these provisions until there have been some test cases. You will need expert advice to pursue any kind of case on these grounds.

Working out your average limit

Some press reporting has suggested that the 48-hour limit applies every week. Except for the special case of night workers involved in dangerous work, this is incorrect. It is always an average limit. So even if you work more than 48 hours one week, if you work fewer the next then you may well have worked less than the 48-hour limit on average.

For most people you calculate your average by looking at your working time over the last 17 weeks. The period over which the average working time is measured is known in the regulations as the 'reference period'. To calculate this you need to add up your total working time for each of the last 17 weeks and then divide by 17.

If you were sick or took leave on any days during this period, you should start counting your reference period a week earlier. You should then include enough extra days from the week after the reference period to make up for days that you did not work during the 17 weeks. If there are not enough extra days then you keep starting the reference period earlier until you have enough to get a full 17-week reference period.

There are some exceptions to the 17-week reference period. In some jobs the time over which the average is worked out is extended to 26 weeks. These are the same groups as shown on page 68, who have reduced rights to choose when they take rest breaks. As with rest break rights, employers can switch to a 26-week reference period when there is an emergency. The reference period for offshore workers is 52 weeks.

If you have not yet worked for a full reference period then you calculate the average from when you started work.

It is also possible to vary the reference period by collective or workforce agreement (see page 69). One way it can be varied is to have successive 17-week blocks as the reference periods rather than have a rolling 17-week period. In other words, the first 17 weeks after an agreement was reached could count as the first reference period. Another reference period would then start in week 18.

Another variation that can be made is to extend the reference period. Unions in some workplaces have agreed deals that extend the reference period to a year, providing what is known as an annualized hours contract. This allows companies to respond to seasonal peaks in demand in a flexible way but ensures employees get extra time off when demand is slack.

Individual opt-outs

At the moment, the 48-hour average limit is the one part of the Working Time Regulations from which individuals can opt out. You need to do this in writing and you can opt out either for a defined period of time or indefinitely.

But you have the right at any time to reverse your opt-out so that you can be covered by the 48-hour average limit once again. The opt-out agreement you signed may have included a time period you have to wait before you are covered again, but this cannot be longer than three months. If there is no time period in your opt-out, then you need only wait seven days.

The commonest abuse of the Working Time Regulations is employers putting undue pressure on their employees to individually opt out of the 48-hour limit. However, they cannot force you to opt out if you do not want to and they are committing an offence if they dismiss you or treat you less favourably than other employees – what the law calls 'detriment'. If they do this, you should take advice, as you are likely to have a strong case at an Employment Tribunal. You will almost certainly get compensation, but you should be aware that if you get the sack tribunals only rarely use their power to get people reinstated to their jobs.

However, you are in a more tricky position if asked at a job interview whether you will be prepared to opt out and it is apparent to you that this is a condition for getting the job. This is clearly against the spirit of the Working Time Regulations, but the regulations do not specifically outlaw it, so employers may be able to get away with this.

Once you have started work with an employer, however, and have signed an opt-out you can give notice to withdraw it at any time. If your employer sacks you at this stage simply for reversing the opt-out, they are breaking the law, and you can take a case to an Employment Tribunal.

You cannot have your basic pay cut to punish you for refusing to opt out. However, if you are paid by the hour, or receive overtime for hours over your basic working week, then you will obviously get more pay if you work more than 48 hours than if you work fewer. There is nothing to stop an employer from paying a higher rate of overtime for hours over 48 hours a week, but if you find your overtime pay has been cut for hours under the 48-hour limit, this may be an illegal variation to your contract of employment. You should take further advice.

All in all, protection against working more than an average 48-hour week is extremely weak in the UK. Knowledge of the law is weak, and employers regularly get away with either ignoring the limit or forcing staff to sign an opt-out. Neither local authorities nor the Health and Safety Executive, which have the enforcement responsibilities divided between them, put any effort into enforcement.

Night working

Rights for night workers are easily summarized:

▪ If you regularly work at nights, you should do no more than an average of eight hours in every 24.

▪ The 48-hour average limit is more strictly regulated, and night workers cannot opt out of the 48-hour average weekly limit (because of the greater threat to your health of night work).

▪ Your employer should provide a free medical check, and, where possible, allow you to switch to other shifts on medical advice.

■ Young people and those doing specially hazardous work get better protection.

However, as with other working time rights, they are not so straightforward in practice. Some groups are exempt, and the averages for night work limits are calculated in a different way than for seeing whether you work more than the 48-hour limit.

Defining night work

If you only occasionally work nights, you do not get this protection; only night workers do. To be classed as a night worker you have to work more than three hours at night as part of the normal course of your job. 'At night' means between 11 pm and 6 am. So if you have an evening shift that finishes at 2 am you are a night worker, but if you finish at 1 am you are not as you are only working two hours at night.

However, this definition of night can be varied by agreement between the employer and the workers by collective and workforce agreements (see page 69). Agreement can also be reached to include more people as night workers – say everyone who works more than two hours during the night period. But there are limits to how much these definitions can be changed. Night time must always be seven hours or more, and it must always include the time between midnight and 5 am.

One of the first court cases under the Working Time Regulations was about the definition of a night worker. The court was asked to rule whether someone who worked one week in three on a night shift was a night worker. The employer argued the worker was not a night worker as she worked days more often than she worked nights, but lost the case. The court ruled she was a night worker and said it was the regular nature of her shift pattern that made her a night worker. However, it is likely that other cases will seek to reopen this issue, and you cannot therefore rely on this case as setting a definite legal precedent.

Working out the average limit for night work

Night work is worked out as a daily average limit, rather than a weekly limit. It is therefore calculated differently from the 48-hour limit. It is important to appreciate that the average is worked out over the days you can legally work in a week, not the days you actually work. As you are only entitled to a 24-hour rest period each week this leaves six days when you can legally work.

In other words, you could work nine hours for five nights each week. At first sight this might look as if it breaks the limit of 'a ceiling of an average of eight hours' night work in every 24'. But you have to include the sixth night, when you could work even though you are not doing so, when you work out the average.

Let's look at that calculation in detail. Your total working hours in a week is 45. To get the average over six days you divide by six. This gives seven and a half hours. You are therefore not over the limit. If you work exactly the same hours each week then you can use this method to see whether you are over the limit. But if your hours vary, then it becomes more complex.

The average is always worked out over 17 weeks. However, those groups of workers who have their 'reference period' extended to 26 weeks for working out the 48-hour limit (see page 68) lose night work hours protection altogether rather than have a longer period for working out the average. If you take time off for holidays or sick leave during the 17-week period, you assume normal hours are worked on those days.

Overtime is only included if it is a regular part of your work and is specified in your contract. If you only work occasional overtime it does not count. If, however, you work overtime every week as part of your normal working pattern, you should include it as part of your total working hours.

If you work different shifts – say one week on nights followed by one week on days – your average night hours will be nowhere near eight hours. We can see why by looking at a two-week period. Say you work five days a week and your night shifts are 10 hours long one week and the day shifts, the next week, are eight hours. Over the two-week period you work 50 hours at night the first week and 40 hours during the day the second week, making 90 hours in all.

But over this period there are 12 days when you can legally work nights. However, as you have only done 50 hours of night work during this two-week period the average is 50 ÷ 12, or 4 hours 10 minutes a day. You are still subject to the 48-hour limit – but you are also below this.

Special hazards

If your work involves special hazards or heavy physical or mental strain, and you are a night worker, then you cannot work more than eight hours in any 24. This is not an average, but an absolute limit. In other words, as soon as you have worked eight hours you must stop. It therefore does apply to split shift workers when they work nights.

But deciding whether your work is covered by this definition may be trickier. Employers and employees together can agree which jobs are covered through a collective agreement – either through union negotiations or a workforce agreement (see page 69). Your employer is also obliged by law to carry out what is called a risk assessment. As part of this they should decide whether any night workers fall under this category.

Exclusions from the eight-hour limit

Both the eight-hour average and the eight-hour absolute limit can be set aside in the same way that variations can be made to the 48-hour limit by collective agreement (see the section on varying the 48-hour week above).

The eight-hour limit does not apply to these jobs and workers:

■ security guards, caretakers and other jobs requiring a permanent presence to protect people and property;

■ where the job involves long travelling distances;
■ where the job requires continuity of service or production such as hospitals, prisons, docks, airports, media, post and telecommunications, civil protection, agriculture;
■ industries where work cannot be interrupted such as utilities;
■ jobs where there are seasonal rushes such as tourism, post and agriculture.

Any night worker can lose this protection if his or her job is suddenly affected by an accident, risk of an accident or other unexpected event. But there is no individual opt-out. You cannot sign away your rights. Even if you want to work more than eight hours on average you cannot, unless you are covered by a collective agreement or fall into one of the groups above.

Health checks

Before you begin night work you should be offered a free health assessment. This should be repeated regularly – the government recommends annually. If night work is bad for your health you should, if it is possible for the employer to do so, be offered a chance to transfer to day work.

A health assessment can take the form of a questionnaire, rather than an examination by a doctor or nurse, as long as the questionnaire has been developed by someone medically qualified and is evaluated by someone with training (but not necessarily a doctor or nurse).

Rights for under-18s

If you are over the school leaving age (16) but younger than 18, you are covered by a different set of European regulations – the Young Workers Directive. These were brought into UK law in the Working Time Regulations. Although your holiday rights are the same as those for older workers, you have different and better rights to breaks.

You should get a continuous break of 12 hours every day (though this can be split in some narrow cases). You should also get a 48-hour continuous break every week (though this can be split in some narrow cases usually involving split shifts, and in some other circumstances limited to 36 hours).

However, as with the 24-hour break enjoyed by older workers, the timing of the break can vary in different weeks. A system where young shop workers got a different two-day break each week would be perfectly legal, for example. You could work 10 days in a row if you had two days' rest at the beginning of the first week and two days off at the end of the second week. In an emergency, and where there is no adult worker available, these breaks can be suspended but the employer must make them up within three weeks.

From April 2003 young workers have not been allowed to work more than eight hours per day or 40 hours in a week. Night work is prohibited. Employers can choose whether 'night' means from 10 pm to 6 am or from 11 pm to 7 am.

However, there are still a number of exemptions: young workers may work longer hours if this is necessary to maintain continuity or production, to respond in a surge in demand, or where no adult is available to do this work. In such cases they must be adequately supervised, their training needs must not be adversely affected, and they must be allowed compensatory rest. In addition, young workers may work at night in hospitals and similar establishments, and if they are employed in cultural, sporting, artistic or advertising activities. They may also work for part of the night, from 10 or 11 pm until midnight, and from 4 am until 6 or 7 am if they are employed in agriculture, retail trading, a hotel or catering business, restaurants or bars, bakeries, or postal and newspaper deliveries.

4

Families and work

Working parents or those with elderly relatives to care for often find it hard to juggle all the competing demands on their time. Much depends on how flexible their employers are prepared to be, but mothers, fathers and carers also have some basic rights in law.

Maternity leave

Working mothers have a range of rights both before and after their babies are born. Maternity rights are very complicated – and the law is not always clear. Here we set out your basic rights, but if you get into difficulties you should check with another source – such as your union or an advice agency. There are contact details at the end of the book. Many employers will provide better rights, which will probably be set out in your contract of employment or staff handbook. They cannot provide a worse deal than the legal minimum even if you have signed a contract that appears to promise less than the law provides.

Pregnancy and maternity leave

The law says employers must not 'unreasonably refuse' pregnant employees paid time off for antenatal care. This is broadly defined and includes antenatal appointments, relaxation and parentcraft classes as well as travelling time. If your employer does unreasonably refuse time off for antenatal care, or if you don't get paid, you can complain to an Employment Tribunal. But the tribunal can only award compensation equal to your pay for the time you took off, or would have taken off.

This is not much use if you did not get your antenatal care. If, however, you do take time off for antenatal care and you are sacked, it is very likely that you could take a case for unfair dismissal. If you are dismissed while you are pregnant, your employer must prove to an Employment Tribunal that you were sacked for a reason that had nothing to do with your pregnancy. This is one of the grounds for unfair dismissal that starts with the first day of your job, even if you were pregnant when you started work. You may also be able to claim sex discrimination.

However, a tribunal cannot guarantee that you will get your job back, and you may not get a very good compensation settlement, although this could be more if you win a sex discrimination case. You should take advice before acting from your union or other advice agency.

Maternity leave entitlement

All pregnant employees are entitled to 52 weeks of maternity leave from the day they start work. You can choose when your maternity leave will begin, but the earliest it can start is 11 weeks before the week the baby is due.

If you are off work for a pregnancy-related reason, such as sickness, in the four weeks before the week in which your baby is due, your employer can insist that your maternity leave start from that date. Many employers don't take this line, though, and would let a woman in this position carry on working until she had originally planned to start her leave.

Every woman who gives birth must have two weeks off (or four if she works in a factory) after the birth. This is compulsory maternity leave and is to protect the health and safety of the mother and the baby.

Giving notice to your employer

In order to qualify for maternity leave you must tell your employer by the end of the 15th week before the baby is due:

■ that you are pregnant;
■ the week in which your baby is expected; and
■ the date when you intend to start your ordinary maternity leave.

You are not obliged to put this notice in writing unless your employer asks you to. However, it is probably a good idea to do this, in case any misunderstandings arise in the future. Also, if your employer requests it, you should provide them with a copy of the maternity certificate (MAT B1) given to you by your GP or midwife. If you are unable to give notice at the 15th week before the baby is due, then you must do so as soon as reasonably practicable.

Once you have told your employer you will be taking maternity leave, they then have 28 days to tell you the date on which your maternity leave ends.

Changing the date your maternity leave starts

After you tell your employer when you intend to start your maternity leave, you can change the date. To do so you must tell your employer of the change at least 28 days before the new or original date, whichever is the earlier.

Terms and conditions while on maternity leave

Although you are entitled to 52 weeks of leave, your terms and conditions are slightly different in the first 26 weeks of leave compared to the second 26 weeks. The first 26 weeks are known as ordinary maternity leave (OML), and the subsequent time off is known as additional maternity leave (AML).

When you are on OML you are entitled to all the benefits you would get if you were still at work, except your wages. Your annual leave will continue to build up, as will any pension that your employer contributes to, and you can continue to use a company mobile phone or car unless your contract forbids this.

Whether or not your contractual terms and conditions continue while you are on AML will depend on what your contract says. You continue to build up statutory paid holiday (20 days, or pro rata for part-timers per year), but unless your contract allows it your contractual holiday entitlements will be suspended. Your employer must continue to make any pension contributions during paid maternity leave, whether AML or OML. At the time of writing, eligible employees (see below) get 39 weeks' paid leave.

Your period of AML counts as continuous employment for working out whether you are entitled to statutory employment rights such as protection against unfair dismissal. But AML only counts as pensionable service for pension schemes that count how long you were employed if your contract or pension scheme rules say so – many do not.

Returning to work after maternity leave

You have the automatic right to return to work following maternity leave, and it is assumed that you will do so unless you say otherwise.

■ You don't have to give your employer notice if you are returning at the end of the full 52 weeks (although it is a good idea to make sure they are expecting you back if they don't contact you).

■ If you decide to return to work earlier than the date notified to you by your employer, then you must give your employer at least 56 days' (eight weeks) notice that you plan to do so. You do not have to give this notice in writing, although it is advisable to do so and keep a copy.

■ Your employer can let you return with less or no notice, although they do not have to, but the most they can make you wait is 56 days (eight weeks) or until the day that your maternity leave was due to end.

■ Your employer does not have to pay you if you turn up for work in the meantime.

If you are returning to work after OML, you have a right to return to the same job. After any AML your employer must provide you with other suitable work if it is not reasonably practicable for you to return to the same job.

If illness prevents you from returning to work

If you are unable to return to work after the end of your maternity leave then you do not lose your right to return but should be treated by your employer as if you have returned to work and are currently on sick leave. You should follow your employer's procedures for sickness. Your employer should treat you in the same way as any other employee who is off sick, including paying you any sick pay that is due to you.

If you decide not to return to work after maternity leave

You should resign in the normal way, giving the notice required by your contract or the notice period that is standard in your workplace. If you do not have a contract, or if nothing has been said about how you should resign, then you should give a week's notice. You do not have to pay back any Statutory Maternity Pay (SMP) you might have received, but you may have to give back any extra pay your employer gave you above the legal minimum.

Other rights

You do have other rights while you are pregnant or on maternity leave:

■ Your employer cannot dismiss you or select you for redundancy for any reason connected with pregnancy or maternity.
■ You should not be treated unfavourably in other ways when you return – having to work inconvenient shifts or having your job downgraded, for example.
■ While you are pregnant, when you have recently given birth and when you are breastfeeding, your employer has to make sure you are not doing work that would put you or your baby's health and safety at risk.

Your contract is likely to set out how your contractual rights will be affected by statutory and additional maternity leave.

Keeping in touch during maternity leave

Your employer may have 'reasonable' contact with you during your maternity leave. What is reasonable will depend on the kind of job you do. It is best to agree arrangements for keeping in touch before you go on leave. Your employer must let you know about any promotion opportunities and other important information while you are away.

You are allowed to work up to 10 days during your leave without losing your right to SMP. This can include keeping-in-touch (KIT) days organized by your employer, but you cannot be required to attend these, nor should you suffer any consequences if you choose not to go. If you do decide to work a KIT day, you need to agree whether or not you will be paid – most employers provide a full day's pay.

Maternity pay and benefits

The rules on maternity pay are complicated and if you are not sure of your entitlements, you should seek advice. You will get SMP for 39 weeks if you meet all the following conditions:

■ you have worked for the same employer for at least 26 weeks by the end of the 15th week before your child is due (this is called the *qualifying week*);

■ you are still in your job in this qualifying week (it does not matter if you are off sick or on holiday);

■ you earn at least the Lower Earnings Limit (before tax) per week on average in the eight weeks (if you are paid weekly) or two months up to the last payday before the end of the qualifying week.

If you do meet those conditions then you are entitled to 90 per cent of your average pay in the first six weeks of maternity leave, and then you will receive the basic rate of SMP for the next 33 weeks, unless your employer is more generous. Many are, and it is likely that your contract of employment will set out the details of your maternity pay.

Maternity Allowance

If you are not entitled to SMP, you may still be entitled to Maternity Allowance, which is also payable for 39 weeks. Maternity Allowance may be payable to you if you have worked for a total of 26 weeks in the 66 weeks before the week your baby is due – although these need not be consecutive weeks. However, you will need to meet some complex earnings conditions and should seek advice from the Department for Work and Pensions or Jobcentre Plus, who will work out how much you should get.

Other benefits

If you are not entitled to SMP or Maternity Allowance, you may be entitled to other benefits such as Incapacity Benefit, and you could also qualify for the new tax credits that have been introduced, including Working Tax Credits and Child Tax Credits. The Sure Start Maternity Grant is available to women on low incomes and you should contact Jobcentre Plus, HMRC or a specialist adviser who will be able to tell you whether you qualify.

Paternity leave

If your partner or spouse is giving birth or adopting a child then you may be entitled to take either one or two weeks of paternity leave. This leave is designed to help you look after them, and can be taken within 56 days of the child being born or being placed in your care. It is available to both same-sex and opposite-sex partners.

Paternity leave entitlement

Where your partner is giving birth

To qualify for paternity leave you must have been continuously employed by your current employer for 26 weeks or more by the end of the 15th week before the child is due – this is known as the *qualifying week*. You must be either the father of the child, or married to or the partner of the child's mother, and you must have responsibility for the child along with the child's mother.

Where your partner is adopting

To qualify for paternity leave you must have been continuously employed by your current employer for 26 weeks or more in the week after the week that your partner is notified that they have been matched with a child – this is known as the *qualifying week*. You must be married to or the partner of the person who is adopting the child and expect to have the main responsibility, along with your partner or spouse, for the child's upbringing.

Giving notice to your employer

Where your partner is giving birth

In the 15th week before the child is expected, you must tell your employer the week that the child is due, how much leave you intend to take (you can take either one week or two consecutive weeks) and the date that you intend the leave to start. There may be cases where it is not possible to give this much notice, for example if a child is born prematurely or a pregnancy is discovered very late. In these circumstances you are allowed to give notice as soon as 'reasonably practicable'.

Your employer can ask to see self-certificate form SC3 *Becoming a parent*, which confirms that you meet all the criteria and so are entitled to take the leave (forms are available from HMRC and can be downloaded from their website www.hmrc.gov.uk), but you only have to give them this certificate if they ask you to. You should ensure you have a copy of it, so that both you and your employer are clear concerning the dates when your leave will start and end. Once your child has been born, you must tell your employer.

Where your partner is adopting a child

In the week after the week in which your partner is told that they have been matched with a child, you must tell your employer the date that your partner was notified; the date that you are expecting the placement to begin; and the date that you want your paternity leave to start. In some cases there might not be time to give this notice, in which case you must give your employer notice as soon as reasonably practicable.

Your employer can ask to see self-certificate form SC4 *Becoming an adoptive parent*, which will confirm that you are entitled to take paternity leave, but you only have to give this to them if they ask. If you do give it to them, keep a copy so that both you and your employer are clear about the dates that your leave will start and end. Once the placement has been made, you must inform your employer of this. Self-certificate form SC4 is available from HMRC and can be downloaded from their website www.hmrc.gov.uk.

Changing the date your paternity leave starts

Even after you have agreed dates for your leave, you can still change your mind and vary the date. You must notify your employer of the change at least 28 days before the new date, or as soon as is reasonably practicable. Your paternity leave will then start on this new date.

Employment terms and conditions while on paternity leave

While on paternity leave, you continue with the same terms and conditions except pay. This is still the case if you take paternity leave and follow it with annual leave or parental leave of less than four weeks (parental leave is discussed later in this chapter).

Returning to work

You are entitled to return to the same job that you had before you went on leave and to benefit from the same conditions that you would have received had you not been on leave. This is the case if you took paternity leave on its own, or linked it with statutory leave such as annual leave or less than four weeks of parental leave.

If you choose to link your paternity leave period with more than four weeks' parental leave then you are allowed to return to the job you were doing before you went on leave, or if your employer can argue that this is not reasonably practicable then you should be given another job that is appropriate for you to do in the circumstances.

Statutory Paternity Pay (SPP)

You will get Statutory Paternity Pay if you meet all the following conditions:

■ You have worked for the same employer for at least 26 weeks by the end of the 15th week before your child is due or the week in which your partner was notified of being matched with a child for adoption.

■ You are still in your job in this qualifying week (it does not matter if you are off sick or on holiday).

■ You earn at least the Lower Earnings Limit (before tax) per week on average in the eight weeks (if you are paid weekly) or two months up to the last payday before the end of the qualifying week.

If you do meet these criteria then you are entitled to receive £100 per week, or £90 per week if your average weekly earnings are less than this. If you are unsure about whether you qualify for paternity pay and leave then it is important that you seek expert advice.

Adoption leave

If you are adopting a child then you are entitled to take up to 52 weeks' adoption leave provided you give proper notice and you meet the eligibility criteria.

In order to get adoption leave you must have been continuously employed by the same employer for 26 weeks or more in the week that you are told you have been matched with a child. This is known as your *qualifying week*. You must be the person adopting the child (in a couple, only one parent can take adoption leave) and you must have notified the adoption agency that you agree to the placement.

Giving notice

You must tell your employer that you want to take adoption leave within seven days of being told by the adoption agency that you have been matched with a child. You must specify the date on which the child is expected to be placed with you and the date that you have chosen your leave period to start.

Your employer can ask for your notice in writing and for evidence that you are entitled to take adoption leave. To provide this you must make available the name and address of the adoption agency; the name and date of birth of the child; the date that you were told that you had been matched with the child; and the date that the agency intends to place the child in your care. This documentary evidence can take the form of a *matching certificate*, which may be available from the adoption agency and is available from the Department for Business, Enterprise and Regulatory Reform at www.direct.gov.uk/en/ Parents. It always makes sense to put these kinds of request in writing and keep copies.

Once you have given your notice, your employer has 28 days to tell you the date on which your adoption leave will finish.

Changing when your adoption leave starts

Once you have told your employer when you intend to start your adoption leave you can change this date. To do this you must tell your employer of the variation at least 28 days before the new date, or as soon as is reasonably practicable. Again, it is best to do this in writing.

Terms and conditions while on adoption leave

Although you are entitled to 52 weeks of adoption leave, your terms and conditions are slightly different in the first 26 weeks – known as ordinary adoption leave (OAL) – than in the subsequent weeks off, known as additional adoption leave (AAL).

When you are on ordinary adoption leave you are normally entitled to all the benefits you would get if you were still at work, except your wages. You will continue to build up holiday and pension rights, for example. You may also be able to continue using a company car or mobile phone although you should check your contract to be sure.

Unless your contract says otherwise, some of your terms and conditions of employment may change during additional adoption leave. You will continue to accrue statutory paid holiday (see Chapter 3), but unless your contract says otherwise any additional contractual holiday entitlements are suspended. Your employer must continue to make any pension contributions you would normally get during paid adoption leave. There is currently an entitlement to 39 weeks' statutory adoption pay for eligible employees (see page 85). AAL does not count as pensionable service but does not interrupt your continuity of service, and the periods of time either side of the AAL period will be treated as continuous. Your period of adoption leave does count as continuous employment for building up statutory employment rights (such as protection against unfair dismissal) but probably won't count for rights provided by your contract of employment. Some of this can be quite complicated and you should seek advice from your trade union representative or a specialist adviser.

Your employer is entitled to maintain 'reasonable' contact with you while you are on adoption leave. Arrangements are the same as for mothers on maternity leave (see page 85).

Returning to work after adoption leave

You have the automatic right to return to work following adoption leave, and it is assumed that you will do so unless you say otherwise.

■ You don't have to tell your employer if you are returning at the end of the full 52 weeks (although it is a good idea to make sure they are expecting you back if they don't contact you).

■ If you decide to return to work earlier than the date specified by your employer then you must give them 56 days' notice of your intention to do so. You do not have to give this notice in writing, although it is advisable that you do and keep a copy.

■ Your employer can let you return earlier, although they do not have to, but the most they can make you wait is 56 days or until the day that your adoption leave was due to end.

■ Your employer does not have to pay you if you turn up for work in the meantime.

If you are returning to work after OAL (the first 26 weeks), you have a right to return to the same job. If you return after a period of AAL (ie more than 26 weeks' leave), your employer is obliged to provide suitable employment if it is not reasonably practicable for you to return to your old job.

If illness prevents you from returning to work

If you cannot return to work on the agreed date then you do not lose your right to return. Instead, your employer should treat you as if you had returned to work but are now on sick leave. You must therefore follow your employer's sickness procedures. Your employer should treat you in the same way as any other employee who is off sick, including paying you any sick pay to which you're entitled.

If you decide not to return to work after adoption leave

You should resign in the normal way, giving the notice required by your contract or that is standard in your workplace. If you do not have a contract, or if nothing has been said about how you should resign, then you should give a week's notice. You do not have to pay back any Statutory Adoption Pay (SAP) you have received, but you may have to give back any extra pay your employer gave you above the statutory minimum.

Other rights

You do have other rights when you are on adoption leave:

■ Your employer cannot dismiss you or select you for redundancy for any reason connected with the adoption.

▪ You should not be treated unfavourably when you go back to work – having to work inconvenient shifts or having your job downgraded, for example.

Statutory Adoption Pay (SAP)

You may be entitled to receive statutory adoption pay while you are on adoption leave. You will receive SAP if you:

▪ are matched with a child by a UK adoption agency;
▪ have been continuously employed by the same employer for at least 26 weeks before the week that you are told you have been matched with a child (it does not matter if you are off sick or on holiday during this time);
▪ earn at least the Lower Earnings Limit (before tax) per week on average in the eight weeks (if you are paid weekly) or two months (if you are paid monthly) up to the last payday before the week after the week you were notified of the child's placement.

You must also provide your employer with the same information that you need to give to trigger adoption leave, contained in the matching certificate described on page 91. You only have to submit it once to your employer, but you must do so at least 28 days before the date that you have chosen your pay period to start, or as soon as is reasonably practicable. If you are in a relationship then your partner may be able to receive paternity pay and paternity leave. However, an individual cannot be in receipt of both statutory adoption *and* statutory paternity pay.

If you qualify for SAP, you will receive either the basic rate or 90 per cent of your average earnings if they are less than the basic rate, for 39 weeks. If you do not qualify for SAP, you may be entitled to other benefits and should contact Jobcentre Plus for this information. Jobcentre Plus information is local and their contact details can be found in your local telephone directory. See Chapter 9 for contact details for HMRC, the

Department for Business, Enterprise and Regulatory Reform, and Citizens' Advice Bureaux.

Parental leave

If you are an employee and have worked for your employer for at least a year, you have the right to take 13 weeks' unpaid parental leave to care for your child. If you are the parent of a child with a disability who qualifies for Disability Living Allowance then you have the right to take 18 weeks' unpaid parental leave.

Some workplaces will have special agreements on parental leave that have been reached between the employer and the union or other workplace representative. For instance, the agreement might set out how and when you can take your leave or it might include some payment for employees taking parental leave. You should check whether any such scheme applies where you work as it will override the basic state scheme.

If your employer does not provide for parental leave payment, you may still qualify for tax credits and benefits. You should consult your local benefits agency and HMRC. You can also speak to a specialist adviser such as a Citizens' Advice Bureau if you are unsure about benefits and tax credits.

You qualify for parental leave if you have parental responsibility for a child or if your name is on the child's birth certificate. Unlike in the case of paid holiday, your employer cannot tell you when to take parental leave but they can postpone it. You can take parental leave:

■ until your child's fifth birthday;
■ in adoption cases, for five years after your child is first placed with you, or until the child's eighteenth birthday if that comes sooner;
■ if your child has a disability and qualifies for Disability Living Allowance (DLA), you can take up to 18 weeks' leave before the child's eighteenth birthday.

Entitlement

You can take 13 weeks' (or 18 weeks' in the case of a child with a disability) leave for each child. You must take the leave in week-long blocks unless your child is in receipt of DLA, in which case you can take it in blocks of a day. You cannot take more than four weeks in any one year for any one child, but if you have more than one child you can take four weeks per year per child.

The entitlement to parental leave is per child and is limited to 13 (or 18) weeks regardless of whether you are with the same employer when you take it. So, if you qualify for parental leave and take four weeks' leave and then move jobs, you will only be entitled to take a further nine (or 14) weeks' leave (per child) once you have reached the qualifying period with your new employer. If during this time your child reaches his or her fifth or eighteenth birthday then you lose your entitlement to parental leave for that child.

Giving notice

You must give 21 days' notice if you want to take parental leave and you must specify the dates when you intend your parental leave to start and finish. You are not obliged to put this notice in writing, but it is often a good idea to do so in case there is any confusion later.

Giving notice of leave that starts with the birth of a child

If you are a father-to-be wanting to take leave from the date of the birth, you should give notice at least 21 days before the beginning of the anticipated week of the birth. You should say when your baby is due and how much leave you want to take once your baby is born. Provided you have given this notice, you can start your parental leave as soon as your baby is born, regardless of whether the birth is earlier or later than was expected.

However, you may decide to take paid paternity leave instead of or as well as unpaid parental leave. You are required to give *28 days' notice* for paternity leave and so if you decide to take paternity leave immediately following a period of parental leave, you should be aware of the different notice requirements and act accordingly. If you are unsure of what to do, you should seek advice. Good employers will provide this information. You can also take parental leave in combination with adoption leave. Take care to follow the notice requirements for each.

Postponement

If an employer thinks that your absence would unduly disrupt the business then they can delay your parental leave for no more than six months after the date that you originally gave. Your employer has to tell you this in writing within seven days from the day you give them notice of your intention to take parental leave, and they have to give you a reason. Your employer cannot postpone your leave entitlement a second time, even if they feel that their reasons for refusing the leave in the first instance have not changed. If you think that your employer has unreasonably postponed your parental leave or prevented you from taking it, you can take your case to an Employment Tribunal. You would have to make your complaint within three months. If this situation occurs then you should seek advice immediately from your union rep or an advice agency.

Returning to work

If you take leave for four weeks or less then you have the right to return to the same job you did before. This is the case if you take parental leave following a different form of statutory leave such as paternity leave, *ordinary* maternity leave or *ordinary* adoption leave.

However, if you take more than four weeks' parental leave on its own, or combined with *additional* maternity leave or *additional* adoption leave, then you have the right to return to the same job unless your employer can demonstrate that it is not reasonably practicable to let you do this. If this is the case then you are entitled to another job that is both suitable and appropriate for you.

Terms and conditions while on parental leave

During parental leave you will still be an employee but your employer is not obliged to pay your wages during that time. Your contractual rights, such as the right to 20 days' paid annual leave, will not be affected and can still build up while you are on parental leave. Your employer, however, can suspend your contractual rights such as any paid holiday above the statutory minimum.

If you took parental leave *before* 6 April 2003 then your employer can leave out the time that you were on leave when calculating seniority or pensionable service. The time spent on parental leave will not count as time employed, but the period of employment before the leave period will be treated as continuous with that following the employee's return to work. However, for employees who have taken parental leave *after* 6 April 2003, periods of parental leave must be counted for purposes of seniority, pension and similar rights. In these circumstances the employee will be treated as if he or she had never been absent.

The other contractual rights that continue automatically are:

■ the notice period stated in your contract – you or your employer should still give this amount of notice if either of you wants to end your job contract;
■ your right to redundancy pay if you are made redundant;
■ procedures for grievance or disciplinary action;
■ any terms and conditions preventing you from working for competing organizations or disclosing confidential information about your employer's business.

Who has parental responsibility?

Natural mothers and married fathers automatically have parental responsibility. Unmarried fathers will have parental responsibility if they have been granted this by the mother or through a court order. For parental leave, an unmarried father whose name appears on his child's birth certificate automatically has parental responsibility. Adoptive parents usually get parental responsibility when the adoption order is made. Same-sex partners and others may sometimes get parental responsibility through legal proceedings.

If your employer is disputing your right to take leave on any of these grounds, you should seek legal advice.

Problems

Your employer must not discriminate against you or treat you unfairly because you apply for or take parental leave. If you feel that you have been discriminated against while on parental leave, you may be able to take a claim to an employment tribunal. If dismissed for seeking or taking parental leave, you would have a case of unfair dismissal.

Some employers give new parents more than the legal minimum of maternity, paternity and adoption leave. If your employer tries to deduct this extra amount from your 13 weeks' parental leave, they could be in breach of your contract, and in certain cases could be guilty of sex discrimination. If any of these problems arise, you should seek advice from your union or a legal specialist.

Flexible working rights for parents and carers

Workers who meet certain conditions now have the right to have a request to work flexibly considered by their employer.

This includes changing your hours, the times when these hours are worked and where you are required to work.

If you need to change your work pattern, you may also have stronger rights under sex discrimination law (see Chapter 6). You would need to take expert legal advice in these circumstances, and you should talk to your union if you are a member.

The new flexible working rights apply to employees who:

■ have 26 weeks' continuous service with their employer at the date that the application is made;
■ are not agency workers;
■ have not made a previous application under the new rights in the past 12 months;

and

■ have a child under six or a disabled child under 18 and:
  - have, or expect to have, responsibility for the upbringing of the child;
  - are making the application in order to care for the child;
  - are parents of the child (including the mother, father, adopter, guardian or foster parent) or are married to the parent or live with the child and the parent in an enduring family relationship (this includes heterosexual and same-sex partners of the parent but not other members of the family).

or

■ are the carer of an adult who is in need of care and:
  - are the spouse, partner, civil partner or relative of the adult in need of care; or
  - live at the same address as the adult in need of care.

Many employers offer better rights on flexible working, and to find out your entitlement you need to check your contract of employment, your staff handbook, or perhaps a special leaflet that the personnel department may provide in larger organizations. Improving benefits and entitlements on flexible working is a priority for unions, so if you work for an organization that recognizes unions, you are very likely to have access to more generous flexible working rights. Any additional rights to flexible working will normally be included in your contract of employment. If this is the case, your employer is legally bound to honour them because they have been promised to you. If you have a dispute over your terms and conditions on flexible working, you should seek specialist advice.

The concept of flexible working is very wide, and you could ask for a variety of different work patterns or arrangements under these new rights. These include:

■ working from home;
■ job-sharing;
■ teleworking;
■ term-time working;
■ compressed hours;
■ flexitime;
■ staggered hours;
■ annualized hours;
■ self-rostering.

How to make a request

You must comply with the following rules when making a request. Your application must:

■ be made in writing, in either paper or electronic form, stating that it is being made under the statutory right to apply for flexible working;
■ confirm your relationship to the child (and, if relevant, to the child's parent) or the adult in need of care;
■ set out your proposed change to your working patterns and explain what effect you think this change would have on your employer and how this might be dealt with;

■ state whether you have made a previous application under this right and, if so, the date on which it was made;
■ be dated.

In addition, if you are a parent your employer must receive your request at least 14 days before the child's sixth birthday or, in the case of a disabled child, the child's eighteenth birthday.

If your request is granted, the terms and conditions of your contract are varied to take account of that change. Unless otherwise agreed, changes to your contract are permanent and *you have no right to revert to your previous terms and conditions.* You should get advice about this from your union representative, if you have one, or a legal adviser. You may want to consider asking for a variation for a specified time period only or, if possible, expressly subject to your right to revert on giving appropriate notice.

Unless your request is granted immediately or you are notified of your employer's agreement within 28 days, your employer must:

■ arrange a meeting with you within 28 days of receiving the application to discuss your request;
■ notify you in writing of their decision within 14 days of the date of the meeting. This notification will either accept the request and establish a start date or other action, confirm an alternative arrangement agreed at the meeting, or reject the request and set out clear business reasons for the rejection, together with notification of the appeals process.

If you decide to appeal, your employer must:

■ arrange to hear your appeal within 14 days of being informed of your decision to appeal;
■ notify you in writing of their decision on the appeal within 14 days after the date of the meeting. This notification will either uphold the appeal, specify the agreed variation and start date, or dismiss the appeal, state the grounds for the decision and contain a sufficient explanation of the refusal.

Your right to be accompanied at meetings

You have the right to be accompanied at meetings or appeal meetings to discuss your request. Your companion must be a fellow worker employed by the same employer as you. You have the right to choose a union representative as your companion if the representative works for the same employer, even if at another site or establishment so long as the overall employer is the same. Your companion is permitted to address the meeting (but not to answer questions on your behalf), and may also confer with you during the meeting. Your employer must allow your companion, whether a union representative or not, a reasonable amount of paid time off work to accompany you.

Your contract of employment or your employer's collective agreement with your union may give wider rights of representation at meetings, and you should check your rights on this carefully. Your employer may also be prepared to allow a union official or other expert on flexible working not employed by the organization to participate in meetings.

If your employer fails or threatens to fail to comply with your right to be accompanied at meetings or appeal meetings, you can complain to an Employment Tribunal. This complaint must in general be made within three months of the failure, or threat of failure, to comply. The tribunal will extend this time limit only if it is satisfied that it was not reasonably practicable for the complaint to have been brought within that period. If you succeed in this claim, you are entitled to an award of compensation of up to two weeks' pay. The upper limit on a week's pay for this purpose is (at the time of writing) £260.

Grounds for your employer refusing your request

Your employer may turn down your request for flexible working only on one or more of a number of 'business' grounds. These are:

- burden of additional costs;
- detrimental effect on ability to meet customer demand;
- inability to reorganize work among existing staff;
- inability to recruit additional staff;
- detrimental impact on quality;
- detrimental impact on performance;
- insufficiency of work during the periods the employee proposes to work;
- planned structural changes.

If your employer turns down your request either initially or after an appeal hearing, they must give in their written notification of refusal a 'sufficient explanation' of why one or more of these business grounds apply. This statement is likely to be important to your case in any subsequent legal proceedings.

Going to an employment tribunal

While the procedure for considering your request is under way, you have the right to complain to an employment tribunal only if your employer has failed to:

- hold a meeting or an appeal meeting; or
- tell you of their decision or appeal decision.

If your request has been rejected on appeal, you may be able to complain to an Employment Tribunal on the wider grounds that your employer:

- failed to comply with the correct procedure as set out earlier in this section;
- rejected your application for reasons that are not on the permitted list of business grounds; or
- based their decision to reject the request on incorrect knowledge of the facts.

Your complaint to an Employment Tribunal must be brought within three months of the date on which you are told of your employer's decision on your appeal or the date on which the breach of procedure was committed. The tribunal will extend this time limit only if it is satisfied that it was not reasonably practicable for the complaint to have been brought within that period.

If the Employment Tribunal finds your complaint to be well founded then it can make a monetary award or order your employer to reconsider your request for flexible working. The maximum award that can be made is only eight weeks' pay, and only up to a statutory limit. This is another reason to find out about any stronger legal rights (with higher potential compensation limits) that you may have as soon as possible.

Instead of an employment tribunal application, you may have the option of choosing binding arbitration of your dispute by an ACAS arbitrator. However, you should be careful about embarking on this course of action, and you should consult your union or legal adviser and ACAS before doing so.

Time off for dependants

All employees have the right to 'reasonable' time off work to help people such as family members or friends who depend on them for assistance in an emergency. There is no set limit on how much time off can be taken but you can only take off the time necessary to sort out the immediate problem.

Your employer can stop your pay while you are away, even if the leave is just a few hours. However, some employers (often those with trade union agreements on 'family', 'special' or 'carers' leave) may give paid leave in these circumstances, perhaps up to a certain number of days per year.

What is a dependant?

A dependant means your parent, wife, husband or child, or someone who lives with you as part of your family. It does not include someone in a more commercial relationship with you, such as a live-in employee or a tenant. A 'dependant' can also be someone who 'reasonably' relies on you for help if he or she is ill or has an accident, or when his or her normal care arrangements have broken down (for example, this could apply to a neighbour or friend of yours with a disability).

Qualifying circumstances

An employee has the right to reasonable time off:

■ to help when a dependant falls ill, gives birth, is injured or assaulted. The definition of illness and injury includes mental illness or injury;
■ when a dependant dies;
■ to cope when the arrangements for caring for a dependant unexpectedly break down;
■ to cope with an unexpected incident involving a dependent child during school hours or on a school trip, or in other circumstances when the school has responsibility for the child.

Employees relying on this right must tell their employer as soon as reasonably practicable why they are absent and (unless they are already back at work) how long the absence is likely to last. This leave is for emergencies or unexpected incidents rather than events that can be predicted. You are expected to take a different form of leave in the latter circumstances.

The right to time off for dependants depends, to a large extent, on what is *reasonable*, and this is not defined in law. Therefore, it can be difficult to know where you stand if your employer refuses you your right to leave or argues that you took unauthorized leave. In this situation you should consult your union rep or a specialist adviser immediately.

These leave rights do not apply to other domestic emergencies such as break-ins, fire or floods, although most employers should be reasonable in such circumstances.

5

Common problems at work

In a well-run workplace it should be possible to resolve problems without involving any legal procedures. Responsible employers will not only have proper internal procedures but also foster the kind of environment where it is possible to raise issues informally. Good employers recognize that if their staff have grievances and other problems they are unlikely to give of their best.

But things can go wrong in even the best-run workplaces. Responsible employers may have good policies, but a bullying manager in a branch office may ignore them all. Of course, you should make every effort to resolve issues informally if it is possible. You can talk to your boss or, if they're the problem, your personnel or human resources department. If you have one, your union representative may well be able to sort out many problems on an informal basis.

In this chapter we look at some of the commonest problems where the law sets standards or could have a role in resolving a problem. These are health and safety, stress, bullying, drink, drugs, smoking and problems with your contract. We end by explaining how the law regulates formal procedures for resolving grievances or disciplinary matters at work.

Health and safety

You have a right to work in a healthy and safe environment. There are tough laws to ensure that your rights in this respect are safeguarded. While there is always room for improvement and a glaring need for more resources for enforcement – as some high-profile cases sometimes remind us – this country is generally recognized as having a relatively effective health and safety regime. However, while most large companies will understand their responsibilities, this is not always the case in smaller companies. And any death or injury at work is one too many.

Under the Health and Safety at Work Act 1974 your employer must ensure that nothing that happens at work makes you ill or injures you (this is known as the 'duty of care'). This could involve guarding machinery, making sure chemicals you work with are safe, and ensuring you can take breaks when you are tired. It even includes providing adequate canteen and toilet facilities.

Every employer must have a health and safety policy, explaining how they will manage health and safety, and who is responsible for what. Your employer must identify the hazards you might face at work, assess the risk these hazards pose and detail the steps that will be taken to prevent those risks.

Many people are confused by the specific legal use of these terms in health and safety. Basically, a *hazard* is something that could cause you harm, and a *risk* is the likelihood of harm arising from the hazard. Hazards can be physical (scaffolding or repetitive work, for example), chemical (eg asbestos or isocyanates), biological (eg tuberculosis) or psychosocial (eg stress).

Under the Act you must cooperate with the steps taken by your employer to protect health and safety in the workplace, to the extent that you are able. So if your employer tells you to work in a certain way because it is safer, they must make it possible for you to do as they say, and you should follow their instructions.

You must not endanger fellow workers by your actions or omissions. Basically, this means you should follow the safety procedures laid down by your managers, where they have given you the appropriate tools and resources. You should also avoid anything that might be seen as 'horseplay' or 'pranks' that could go wrong and cause injury or illness.

There are also 'implied' rights and duties in your contract of employment (see Chapter 1) which can be important in any tribunal or court case. Again, there is a basic duty for your employer to provide a safe and healthy workplace, and for you to pay proper regard in the workplace to your own and your colleagues' health and safety.

No goggles provided

Sheila Robinson and her fellow employees were required to wear eye protectors while at work. Sheila was given goggles, but they were no use because she had to wear glasses. She complained to the safety officer and he said he would approach the company to see if they would pay for special eye protectors fitted with Sheila's prescription lenses. But she heard nothing more about the matter and after more than a year decided that she was left with no alternative but to resign.

Sheila claimed that she had been constructively dismissed and that the dismissal was unfair. She won, though only after an appeal. The Employment Appeal Tribunal ruled that the employer was in breach of their common law duty to take reasonable care for the safety of employees. It was held that this general duty included an obligation to act promptly and reasonably in dealing with safety questions or complaints. It was found that there was no good reason for the employer's failure to respond to the complaint, and so the constructive dismissal was found to be unfair.

Everyone is covered

Statutory health and safety rights are not limited to employees (see the Introduction for the difference between employees and other legal categories of worker). Anyone present in the workplace is covered, whether they are an employee or a worker – including agency and sub-contracted workers. Even visitors and others not directly under the control of the employer are protected.

A special government agency called the Health and Safety Executive (HSE) polices health and safety. If an accident occurs or if workers, unions or a member of the public raise serious concerns with the HSE, it will investigate and can order changes to be made. As a final resort it can close a dangerous workplace down and prosecute employers in the criminal courts.

In addition, if you are injured at work because of a failure by your employer to maintain proper standards you can claim compensation in a civil action in a county court or the High Court (see pages 183–84). Employers must be insured against such claims, and should display the certificate.

Your employer must provide you with information about the risks and hazards of your work, and what they intend to do about them. They must provide you with training (at no cost to you) in how to work safely, and keep your training up to date.

Hazardous chemicals are required by law to come with a Safety Data Sheet setting out what the hazards are, and what can be done to prevent illness and injury. The supplier is legally obliged to supply these sheets to your employer.

What your employer must do

Every employer must conduct a risk assessment, and then follow a legally binding 'hierarchy of control' which lays down the order in which various steps should be taken to deal with risks to their staff or anyone else at their workplace. This hierarchy is laid out in the Management of Health and Safety at Work Regulations 1999.

Firstly, the source of the risk should be replaced – for example, different machinery, chemicals or processes could be introduced.

Secondly, and only if the first option is not possible or 'reasonably practicable', the source of the risk should be isolated from you and your fellow workers. For example, it could be put in a sealed room, or guards could be put on machinery.

Thirdly, if the first two steps cannot be taken, the risk should be minimized, by using less of a substance, or reducing the time you are exposed to the risk.

Lastly, if all else fails, the employer should provide you with personal protective equipment (such as ear-plugs, overalls and breathing apparatus).

Most health and safety law requires employers to take all the steps that are 'reasonably practicable'. This means that they do not have to use a sledgehammer to crack a nut. But it does not mean that if it costs money they do not have to do it, and it does not even mean that if they cannot afford it they do not have to do it. In practice, most health and safety measures pay for themselves in reduced accidents, reduced sick pay and reduced compensation payments.

At a minimum, your employer must:

■ maintain plant and work systems safely;
■ ensure that risks to health and safety are avoided when using, handling, storing or transporting substances or articles;
■ provide information, training and supervision to ensure health and safety of workers;
■ maintain safe access to and from the workplace;
■ prepare a statement of general policy on health and safety; ensure that minimum standards are met and bring these to workers' attention;

▪ ensure that there are workforce safety representatives and consult with them so that they can assist in establishing and maintaining health and safety standards;
▪ set up a safety committee to review arrangements if the safety representatives request this.

If a union is recognized in your workplace, the safety reps will be chosen through union channels. Where there is no union, it is up to the employer to ensure there are workplace safety representatives, unless it is a small firm employing fewer than five. Such small companies are still covered by health and safety law, but there is no requirement for safety reps.

Where unions are fully involved in the workplace health and safety system, accident rates fall by more than 50 per cent. Whenever your employer does something that could affect your health and safety, they are required by law to consult either your safety representative or the workers who are affected. This consultation must be genuine – it must be 'in good time' (legal jargon that means it cannot be left so late that there would be no time to make changes as a result of the consultation), and your employer must take account of your response.

Where there is union recognition, unions can appoint safety representatives who have a right to time off for union training; a right to be consulted and to represent their fellow workers; a right to investigate accidents and a right to be involved in inspections by the HSE or local environmental health officers. They can also require joint union–management safety committees to be set up, which have the backing of the national union – providing them with access to information and back-up.

If you have a problem at work regarding health and safety, the first person to contact should be your supervisor or manager. If you are not satisfied with the response or are unsure about your position or what to do, contact your safety representative. You should be given his or her name and location when you join the company, probably in a staff handbook or attachment to your contract of employment, and it will most likely be posted up somewhere on a notice board.

These rules are general and there have naturally been arguments about how they apply in practice. There is a range of case law, however, which specialist advisers will be able to help you with. We describe some specific issues below.

Special hazards

In addition to these general rights and responsibilities there are many detailed rules and regulations about particular hazards that will affect different workplaces or occupations, such as offshore oil or quarrying. These cover issues such as handling particular chemicals, working with particular machinery, noise at work, or where there is a risk of electric shock. Normally there is a duty to display these regulations or make them available. Although they are often in rather heavy legal language and usually presented in extremely dull small print, it is worthwhile studying them.

Some of the areas covered by specific legislation (or where legislation is being considered) are:

■ **Back strain** – the Manual Handling Regulations cover most hazards to the back, including heavy lifting (although there are no maximum weights) – the Display Screen Equipment Regulations cover back problems caused by visual display units (VDUs).

■ **Stress** – the general duties of employers to care for their employees and to assess risks apply, and the HSE (Health and Safety Executive) has developed standards on managing stress at work (see pages 115–18 for more on stress).

■ **RSI (Repetitive Strain Injury)** – the Display Screen Equipment Regulations cover using VDUs, and the Management of Health and Safety at Work Regulations cover the need to assess risks (including RSI).

■ **Noise** – if you are exposed to more than 80dB (decibels) at work, your employer should be reducing the noise levels or at least giving you protection – the Noise at Work Regulations cover the issue.

■ **Asbestos** – exposure to asbestos kills more people than any other work-related hazard. The Control of Asbestos at Work Regulations 2006 set out your employer's duties.

■ **Temperature** – there are minimum legal temperatures in the Workplace (Health, Safety and Welfare) Regulations, but only guidance about maximum temperatures (in the Health and Safety Executive's *Working in the Comfort Zone*).

■ **Asthma** – workplace exposure to chemicals that cause asthma is covered by the Control of Substances Hazardous to Health (COSHH) Regulations and the HSE has appended an Approved Code of Practice on asthma itself to the COSHH Regulations.

There are also specific requirements relating to the provision of first aid facilities and to the reporting of accidents at work or the occurrence of serious illnesses at work. For more details, contact your union or the Health and Safety Executive (address at the back of the book).

If you work in a unionized workplace, it is likely that the union will have made a number of agreements on health and safety issues over and above the statutory minimum. These might include issues such as lifting heavy weights or the temperature in your workplace.

If you believe that you are being put into a dangerous situation at work and there is a 'dangerous and imminent risk' to you or fellow workers, you have the right to stop work and leave the area. If your employer disciplines you, you can apply for compensation, or reinstatement if you are sacked. Before walking off the job you should, unless there really is no time, raise your concerns first with your manager and/or safety representative or union representative.

If the worst happens

Despite all the regulations, the work of the Health and Safety Executive and union action, 2 million people are injured at work every year and many more suffer a work-related illness.

This is what you should do if you are injured or made ill by your work.

Firstly, report it to your line manager and/or safety representative. Get him or her to record it in the accident book. If you suffer some specified injuries and illnesses, your employer must tell the HSE. This does not necessarily trigger an inspection, but does allow the HSE to know what is happening in workplaces.

Secondly, or if you have problems with the first step, see your GP and explain how your work caused your injury or illness, and, if you are a member, tell your union. If appropriate, your GP or your employer may provide rehabilitation, such as physiotherapy, to get you back to fitness and back to work.

If your injury or illness causes you to lose wages, or causes pain and disability for more than a few weeks, you may be able to claim benefits from Jobcentre Plus, or compensation from your employer. If the injury was due to criminal violence, tell the police. You may be able to claim from the Home Office criminal injuries compensation scheme.

Stress at work

Stress at work has been described as the new workplace epidemic. Every so often a spectacular case hits the headlines when someone wins a substantial award as compensation for suffering stress at work. But such cases are relatively rare, the more common reality is that workers are suffering in silence as stress levels rise each year. Many factors can add to stress levels. Long hours, exposure to noise, a heavy workload, little or no control over the pace of work and poor management are just some of the common contributory factors.

If you do feel that workplace stress is damaging your health then speak to someone about it. It can be your line manager, steward or, if you have one, a workplace human resources officer, but if you continue working in that environment it is likely to make you even more ill.

If you are suffering from a stress-related illness such as depression and anxiety, remember that the worst thing you can do is nothing. Make sure that you speak to your doctor. There are treatments available that can help people recover from a stress-related illness.

Although there is no recognition of stress in UK employment law, that does not mean that you cannot look to the law for help. In severe cases workers, supported by unions, have been able to seek compensation from their employer.

Over 6,000 new cases of work-related stress are taken on by union solicitors each year, a statistic that should wake employers up to the consequences of ignoring stress in their workplace. The first step is to try to identify the factors that are causing you to be stressed, as some are regulated in their own right.

If long hours are the cause then you should check whether you are working longer than the Working Time Regulations allow (see Chapter 3). If noise levels are a problem, then you should talk to your safety representative. Your hearing may also be in danger, and you should take urgent action.

If the real cause of your stress is your heavy workload then you should talk to your manager to see if he or she can take steps to relieve the burden. Many managers have little idea how long tasks they set can take. You should make sure they do. If they are not prepared to take the issue seriously and try to work through with you what needs to be done, then you should ask them directly to take specific action to reduce your stress level. You are always best advised to put this in writing, and take notes of any discussion or write it up as soon as possible afterwards.

If your manager still refuses to deal with your problem, you should consider a formal grievance procedure if your employer has one (see pages 130–134 for more about grievance procedures).

If your stress gets to the point where it is making you ill or you really feel you cannot cope, you should go and see your GP and explain the problem. He or she will probably be willing to sign you off sick for a period of time. This may well bring the issue to a head. One can hope that this will persuade your employer that there is a serious problem and that something needs to be done about it. On the other hand, they may take action against you for absenteeism or 'under-performance' or for some other symptom of your stress.

If your employer takes action against you or continues to ignore your problem, you may have the basis of a court case, and you should seek advice. Your case might be that your employer is in breach of the implied duty in the contract of employment to provide a healthy and safe working environment for you. If you are stressed and tired, you are likely to be a hazard to yourself and other workers.

If you are dismissed, or feel that you simply cannot take any more and walk out, you may be able to claim constructive dismissal on the grounds that the situation made it impossible for you to continue working (see Chapter 7 for more about constructive dismissal). It is, however, hard to win constructive dismissal cases. You will almost certainly need to be able to show that you did everything possible to resolve the issue, including using any internal formal procedures, before you left your job.

Tackling the causes

There is no easy individual solution to workplace stress other than to tackle its causes. Research shows that it is not just the amount of work you have to do that leads to stress, but how much control you have over the pace of your work. Anything that gives you more control over how you work will help reduce stress levels.

This is an area where unions can usually achieve more than workers acting on their own. It is likely that other workers are also suffering. A union can present a joint case and approach the employer without any need for you to be personally involved – which is only likely to add to your stress levels.

Macho-management is often a cause of stress. A workplace where a union has helped foster a spirit of partnership is far less likely to rely on top-down management. Giving employees more control over their own workloads reduces pressure and stress, and usually leads to people working more effectively.

Never forget that stress is avoidable, and the Health and Safety Executive have produced detailed guidance for employers on how to tackle it. These are contained in their Management Standards. Tackling stress does however require a long-term commitment from management and an acceptance, from the top, that things must change.

Other problems at work

Bullying

A TUC poll discovered that 5 million people in Britain have been bullied at work. It can be a difficult issue to deal with, but if you are being bullied at work, either by your employer, a line manager or by a fellow worker, do not suffer in silence.

The basic legal protection you have against bullying, as with stress, is the implied duty in your contract of employment of your employer to protect you from any actions in the workplace which cause you ill health or put your safety at risk. This includes action taken by other workers.

Serious bullying can clearly do both these things. But less serious bullying should also be unacceptable as it can often grow into more substantial bullying if left unchecked. If your workplace has a grievance procedure you should use this. If it does not you should make a formal complaint in writing to your line manager. If he or she is the bully, go above his or her head, or go to your personnel or human resources department if there is one. If you are being bullied you should keep a diary of all the incidents, the effect they have on you and anything that you do to raise the issue. This will provide the evidence you need, especially if you can produce other witnesses.

If none of this works, you may be able to pursue a claim in court, using similar arguments to a stress case that your employer has failed to provide a safe and healthy working environment.

If the bullying involves an element of sex, race or disability discrimination or harassment then the law is more clear, and you can probably make a complaint to an Employment Tribunal (see Chapter 6).

Drink and drugs

Alcohol and drug misuse can cause a range of problems at work. At one end is the genuine concern that people involved in dangerous or potentially dangerous activities such as driving a train, flying a plane or using dangerous machinery are not under the influence of any intoxicating substance. At the other end is an invasion of individual privacy. What you do in your spare time, as long as it has no effect on your ability to do your job, should not generally be of concern to your employer. If you are having problems with drink or drugs, you should seek specialist help. Some suggestions are given in Chapter 9.

While drugs throw up immediate problems because of their illegality, it is probably true to say that alcohol causes more work-related problems. But both can be a real hazard in the workplace, not just to you, but to your colleagues as well.

Although many people can function perfectly well at their jobs after a glass of wine or beer with their lunch, it is not unreasonable for employers to expect their staff to be clear-headed while at work. On the other hand, they should also realize that stress and other work-related problems can be the prime cause of drink and drug dependency.

Alcohol misuse

Sensible employers will have proper policies for dealing with drink problems. About the worst way of dealing with alcoholism is ignoring it until it is too late. But it is easy for well-meaning colleagues, and even management, to turn a blind eye as a drink problem deteriorates to the point where the only option is dismissal due to chronic bad health, unreliability or other symptoms of alcohol dependency.

Many still see alcohol misuse as a personal failing – behaviour that shows a lack of moral fibre. In fact, it is often the diligent, conscientious worker who can no longer cope who misuses alcohol.

You will probably know if you have a problem with alcohol. This is a book about your rights at work and you should look elsewhere for advice on sensible drinking, but your employer would almost certainly have a good case for dismissing you for gross misconduct if you were routinely drunk or drinking at work, as long as the rules were applied fairly and uniformly across the workforce.

If your job involves the safety of others – for example, driving a bus, train or plane – drinking will be strictly prohibited in your contract of employment, not just during working hours, but also for a set period before you begin each period of work, as alcohol remains in the body for some time after drinking. If your contract of employment prohibits alcohol, under the Health and Safety Act, you are entitled to a copy of your employer's policy on alcohol in the workplace. If your employer intends to introduce such a policy your employer is required to consult 'in good time' with their workforce, or union representatives, on the implications of the policy and how staff will be expected to comply with it.

However, automatic dismissal is not necessarily the best approach. A better way is for both you and your employer to recognize that you have a drink problem. In return for you seeking treatment or help in giving up or cutting down to sensible levels of social drinking, your employer should be prepared to provide support and some understanding that such problems cannot be solved overnight.

Ideally there should be ways of recognizing and dealing with a drink problem before it causes a breakdown in the employment relationship or leads you to do something that in itself would be likely to result in disciplinary action. If you believe that you are misusing alcohol, you should seek help before it causes problems with your employer. If you let the problem get worse, it will start to affect you at work.

Some companies have an occupational doctor or nurse, or a welfare officer, who would be able to provide confidential help. If you are in a union, it may be able to help. Otherwise, you should seek assistance from your GP or from one of the organizations like Alcohol Concern, which are listed at the back of this book. They will try to establish why you are drinking too much. Work-related stress or other problems can be a factor that leads to drink problems. As we have seen earlier in this chapter, employers do have a duty of care and should not subject their staff to excess stress. This is one reason why they should not automatically deal with drink-related problems as a disciplinary matter. Poor employment practices may have triggered the problem in the first place.

Drug misuse

Many of the problems associated with the misuse of drugs at work are similar to those associated with the misuse of alcohol and the ways in which you can tackle the problem are also similar.

However, the most obvious *difference* is that alcohol is legal, while most recreational drugs are not. Your employer is perfectly within their rights to call the police if you are caught in possession of illegal drugs at work. You could be both prosecuted and dismissed for gross misconduct.

The Misuse of Drugs Act 1971 classifies drugs in three categories, A, B and C, according to their relative harmfulness when misused. Class A includes LSD, cocaine, heroin, morphine, methadone, opium, ecstasy and injectable forms of Class B drugs; Class B includes amphetamines ('speed'), barbiturates ('downers'), codeine and methaqualone ('Mandrax'); Class C drugs include most sleeping pills, tranquillizers, cannabis and some of the less harmful amphetamines. Glue and solvents are not controlled by the Act but when inhaled or sniffed cause extreme perceptual distortion and risk of heart failure and brain damage. Most employers would be likely to include solvent misuse under the general heading of drug misuse.

Some employers now use random testing in the workplace to help them to identify drug misuse. If this is included in your contract of employment then your employer can almost certainly dismiss you for refusing to provide a sample. If, however, your contract does not permit drugs testing then you are in something of a legal grey area.

If you have worked for more than a year, it might well constitute unfair dismissal if you were sacked simply for refusing to provide a sample for a drugs test. The new right to privacy in the Human Rights Act may also give you some protection from your first day at work. This, however, is a new law and there will need to be some test cases before anyone can be certain that you have any protection in this area. As we said in Chapter 1, you can refuse to provide a drugs sample at a job interview but there is nothing to stop your potential employer rejecting you for the job if you do.

As with alcohol, you should ask for a copy of your employer's policy on drugs in the workplace. Depending on the method the employer uses to hold the results of your test, the employer may need to comply with the Data Protection Act. You are entitled to medical privacy so make enquiries of your employer about the security of such information in the processes used by the employer and their testing laboratory services.

If you are unsure about the methods being used by your employer contact your union, your local Health and Safety Executive office or one of the alcohol and/or drugs advice agencies at the back of this book.

Another tricky area is whether your employer can take action against you at work if you are prosecuted or cautioned for a drugs offence committed outside work and when there is no argument that drug-taking has affected your ability to do your job. Whether your employer, the government or unions like it or not, very many employees do take illegal recreational drugs.

Whether you can claim unfair dismissal will depend on a number of factors if you are sacked as a result of a drugs offence outside work. An important one will be the nature of the job you do, and whether your offence will impact on your employer's reputation. To take an extreme example, if your job is promoting an anti-drugs message then it would be hard to claim unfair dismissal if you are sacked for using drugs. If you are carrying out a routine job then you may have a better chance. You will need to seek advice.

If you are using prescribed drugs at work that could, if misused, be dangerous, you may want to consider letting your employer know, though you are under no obligation to do this.

Organizations that can give advice on drugs are listed in Chapter 9.

Smoking

There can be no doubt that smoking is not just bad for your health, but for anyone who has to breathe your smoke. But those who smoke are usually addicted to smoking and find it difficult to go for long periods without a cigarette. Non-smokers, on the other hand, often find it objectionable as well as potentially hazardous to their health.

That is why Parliament voted to ban smoking in workplaces and all public places from July 2007, with a small number of exemptions. However, tensions can remain over smoking outside and smoking breaks. Good employers have followed up the ban with help for staff who want to give up.

Contractual problems

Your contract of employment sets out the terms under which you are employed. Your employer should not make changes to your contract unless you agree to them. However, if you disagree with them but accept them in practice by following the changes then the law says that you have accepted them and you lose the right to object. So, if your employer tells you that you must now work an extra half-hour a day, you must continue to leave work at your old time if you are to resist the changes successfully. This is because the courts can find a contract to have changed by custom and practice. In other words, if you do your job in a particular way for some time but then try to go back to working the way set out in writing in your contract of employment, you would be likely to lose in any legal process. A tribunal or court would rule that your contract of employment had changed by custom and practice.

Changes to your contract of employment may be made through an agreement between your employer and a recognized union (see Chapter 1). This may affect you even if you are not a member of the union if the union's agreement covers all workers in the workplace, or all workers on your grade.

If your employer wants to change the terms of your contract, they must give you a statement setting out the new conditions and asking you to accept them. If you do not agree and the change is implemented in any case then you can ask a civil court to rule that the employer is in breach of contract and sue for restoration of the original terms or damages. You cannot go to an Employment Tribunal for breach of contract claims, unless you have been dismissed, or have left your job, as a result (see Chapter 8).

You are only likely to succeed in a claim if the change has fundamentally altered the contract. Examples where the courts would be likely to rule in your favour include reducing your wages or changing your retirement age. An example of a change where you would probably lose any claim would be if you were asked to move to a new type of computer. This would not normally constitute a fundamental change.

If you believe that the change is so fundamental that it makes it impossible for you to continue working, you can resign and claim constructive dismissal, although this is always risky (see Chapter 7).

If your employer gives you notice that they intend to change your contract, the law will see this as terminating your current contract and offering you a new one. This means that if you do not want to work under the new terms you may be able to claim unfair dismissal. A tribunal is unlikely, however, to find for you unless the changes are pretty radical (see Chapter 7).

A move too far?

Mr Aslam worked for a bank in Leeds on a low salary. His contract contained a clear mobility clause that stated that he could be transferred to any of the bank's workplaces in the UK. Mr Aslam was told to move to the bank's Birmingham branch without notice but he refused on both financial and personal grounds (he was offered no relocation expenses, and his wife had just suffered a miscarriage). The bank asserted that it had a clear right to insist on the transfer under the express mobility clause of Mr Aslam's contract. He resigned, claimed constructive dismissal and won.

The employer argued that they had simply invoked an explicit clause of the contract, but this was rejected. The EAT ruled that employers still have to meet the implied terms in any contract, and in particular when dealing with mobility clauses: reasonable notice must be given before exercising the power to transfer an employee; a mobility clause must be operated in a way to make it feasible (an employee should not be required to do something that was, in practice, impossible). Also, a mobility clause is subject to a general duty not to behave in a way likely to destroy mutual trust and confidence between employer and employee.

In the same way that an employer is not entitled to apply a rule in any way they want, they are similarly not entitled to insist on a contractual right in any way they want. In both cases there is a duty of reasonableness.

Disciplinary procedures

If you get into trouble at work, or your employer thinks that you are not working effectively, it is likely that your employer will start a formal disciplinary procedure. Unless you are guilty of serious misconduct or your employer is unfair, it is likely that this first stage of the procedure will end with you being given a verbal warning. Responsible employers will view a first stage as an opportunity to encourage you to improve your performance rather than punish you.

All employers, whatever their size, now have to have minimum procedures in place for dealing with disciplinary action and dismissal. These are known as the statutory dispute resolution procedures and also mean that all employers must have a grievance procedure, though the rules are likely to change in 2009.

ACAS (the Advisory, Conciliation and Arbitration Service) has produced a good model disciplinary procedure, which many employers use. You must be told about the disciplinary procedure in your contract, in a staff handbook or in your written statement of employment particulars (see Chapter 1). In the public sector and larger private companies, disciplinary and grievance procedures are almost always available. A tribunal will accept a less formal procedure in a small company as fair, but will still expect it to allow you to give your point of view and follow some basic principles as set out in the statutory procedures (see Chapter 8 for more about this).

The disciplinary procedure must be set out in writing and you should receive a copy of it, or at least be told where you can get a copy, when you start work. Normally, a disciplinary procedure will have a number of stages of increasing seriousness. But your employer can dismiss or suspend you on the spot if you are guilty of a serious offence. Normally, this will be called 'gross misconduct'. Examples of gross misconduct offences are often contained in your contract of employment or the disciplinary procedure itself. They are likely to include offences such as assault, theft and workplace drug abuse.

If you are not accused of gross misconduct the first stage is likely to be a verbal warning. Your manager or another senior member of staff will call you in and tell you that you must improve your performance, or not continue to do something wrong. You could, for example, be told that you must stop being late for work. The warning is usually lifted if your conduct improves. The employer should tell you that the warning is formal and is the first part of the disciplinary procedure.

The next stage is likely to be a written warning, if you do not improve your performance. If the offence is regarded as more serious, your employer may go straight to this stage without giving a verbal warning. The written warning should give details of the complaint against you, the improvement required and the timescale allowed for the improvement. The warning should notify you that if there were no improvement, your employer would invoke the next stage of the procedure. Generally, if there is an improvement, the written warning will be removed from your file after a year.

There may be provision for a final written warning, which can be the last stage before dismissal. This warning must tell you that dismissal is the next stage and also tell you about any appeal procedure. Again, it is likely that the warning would be kept on your file for at least a year.

Where the possible outcome of the disciplinary procedure is demotion, reduction in pay or dismissal, your employer must tell you to attend a disciplinary hearing. You have a legal right to be accompanied by a trade union representative or official, or a workplace colleague (see below). You are strongly advised to exercise that right and to choose somebody who has had past experience of handling disciplinary hearings in your workplace. If you, or your chosen representative, cannot attend at the time or date given, you have a legal right to ask for a postponement of up to five days, and for a rearranged hearing at a different time and date. Your employer should send you a statement setting out what you have done, or failed to do, that might result in disciplinary action or dismissal.

At the hearing, your employer will explain why you have been asked to attend. You or your representative will then be invited to make an opening statement so that you can explain your behaviour or refute the charge, depending on the circumstances. You will probably be allowed to call witnesses in your support. But you should make sure that they understand why they are being called and what they are being asked to do. You should not ask anyone to do anything but tell the truth, but it is perfectly legitimate to talk through with him or her what he or she will say to ensure it is helpful. You can be sure your employer is doing the same with the witnesses they are likely to call. It is important to prepare your case carefully and be sure of all your facts. You should do this with the person who will be accompanying you. Think through what is likely to be said against you and how best you can respond to it. For example, it may be better to present your case in a way that suggests your accuser has made an honest mistake (if this is consistent with the facts).

A formal disciplinary hearing, particularly in a larger company, is likely to be before more than a single manager. It could, for example, comprise a senior manager, the personnel or human resources manager and your line manager or supervisor.

After the hearing, your employer will let you know, probably both verbally and in writing, what has been decided. This could be dismissal, with appropriate notice, or, if agreed by you or provided for in your contract, payment in lieu of notice. Dismissal decisions should only be taken by senior managers. Other penalties might be transfer, suspension with or without pay, demotion or loss of increment, but only if such penalties are allowed for in your contract or agreed by you.

The written notification of the penalty should include the reasons. If you are dismissed and have been employed by your employer continuously for one year or more, you have a statutory right to written reasons for dismissal (see Chapter 7).

Your employer must also inform you of your right of appeal. You will probably have to lodge your appeal within a certain, probably short, time, often five working days. The appeal should be heard by a senior individual not previously involved in the disciplinary procedure. In a small business this may not be possible. Again, you have a right to be accompanied by your union representative or by a colleague. It is likely that you or your representative will be invited to open the proceedings by explaining why you are appealing against the decision to discipline or dismiss you. You should get a verbal decision, followed by a written decision, on the same day, or as soon as possible after this.

Failure by your employer to use the procedure properly will count against them if you make a subsequent claim at an Employment Tribunal and can lead to an increase in any compensation you are awarded. If you fail to attend a hearing, unless it is for good reason, your compensation can be reduced even if the tribunal finds the dismissal to have been unfair (see Chapter 8).

It may be that your employer has more than one complaint about you. If so, each should be treated as a separate issue, particularly when establishing whether they are justified or not. However, if it comes to deciding a penalty for multiple offences it is legitimate for your employer to consider them together.

In practice, many employers will put complaints together and deal with them in one procedure and at one hearing. If this is the case, you should insist that each offence be dealt with individually. You should not allow your employer simply to create a general impression of your alleged failures as a substitute for a proper investigation of the facts in each case.

A criminal prosecution outside the workplace should not automatically trigger a disciplinary procedure, though when this can occur may be specified in your contract. If, for example, you are prosecuted and found guilty of an offence against children and you are employed in a job that involves working with children, you must expect a disciplinary procedure at work.

A criminal prosecution for an offence committed in the workplace is likely to trigger dismissal for gross misconduct, depending on the nature of the offence. Your employer, however, should not rely on an outside process. They should still conduct their own investigation regardless of the criminal prosecution. You may be suspended pending the criminal investigation. This should be on full pay until the case is decided, unless your contract provides otherwise.

A fight to the finish?

Jason Green was involved in an argument with his supervisor. During the argument the supervisor questioned the fidelity of Jason's wife, and Jason punched the supervisor. He was sacked. The employer argued that this was an inevitable consequence of striking a superior. But Jason claimed unfair dismissal, and won.

The tribunal did not agree with the employer that dismissal was the inevitable consequence of Jason's action. The degree of provocation should be looked at, and Jason had acted under severe provocation.

However, this should not be taken as a green light to hit your boss! There are very few cases where anyone has won an unfair dismissal case after striking a manager.

Grievance procedures

Do not confuse these with disciplinary procedures! These are used where your employer believes that you have done something wrong, or are not performing well. Grievance procedures are for use where *you* have a grievance or a complaint about something that is happening at work. In other words disciplinary procedures are when your employer thinks you are doing something wrong. Grievance procedures are for when you think *you* are the victim.

There is currently a legal requirement for your employer to have a grievance procedure. You must be given information about it when you start work. This can be either in your staff handbook or provided with your contract or statement of written particulars of employment. You must use it before taking a Tribunal case.

You will probably not be entitled to trigger a grievance procedure for a relatively trivial issue, such as being mildly irritated by your neighbour's habit of chewing gum all day. But you should be free to raise any more serious matter. This may be a complaint about something your employer or manager is doing or not doing, or a complaint about the conduct of another member of staff that you believe your employer should stop. Issues that you should be able to raise at a grievance procedure include bullying, impossible deadlines, sexual, racial or any other kind of harassment, or seriously uncomfortable working conditions.

Some grievances indicate the development of serious general workplace issues, relating to health and safety or sex discrimination. Others may only be serious for you. In either case, good employers will take any grievance seriously unless investigation confirms them as minor matters.

Details will differ from workplace to workplace but under the statutory procedure you will need to put your grievance in writing to your immediate supervisor or line manager to trigger the procedure. An effort may be made at this stage by your employer to resolve the matter more informally; indeed, you may have lodged the grievance as a way of underlining its seriousness but with the aim of settling the issues informally. If you think this is a genuine effort then it may be appropriate to cooperate, but if you think it is simply a time-wasting dodge or a way of excluding your representative then insist on a formal hearing.

If you have a trade union representative he or she will be able to help and advise you about the best way of bringing a successful grievance procedure. He or she will also be able to accompany you at the formal hearing, as you have the same representation rights as at a disciplinary hearing (see below for more details).

The formal grievance hearing will probably take place before one or more senior managers, probably with someone from your personnel or human resources department. It will be up to you to make your case. Procedures vary from organization to organization, but you will almost certainly be allowed to present written evidence in support of your case and you may be able to call witnesses. If, for example, you were complaining about the stress caused by a heavy workload then a letter from your doctor would help. If you are complaining about harassment, then, if there are any witnesses, you should aim to call them or present written statements from them. You should receive the result of the hearing as soon as possible. Good practice would be to let you have a written ruling within five working days.

If you are not happy with the result then you should be able to raise it again with a more senior manager at an appeal stage. Another shorter hearing may well take place, depending on the nature of the grievance. Again, you have the right to be accompanied.

If you still do not get a satisfactory response, in a larger company there may be provision for a further full grievance hearing, involving the most senior manager in the organization or plant, and even a further appeal stage beyond that. Again, in the final hearing and at the appeal, depending on the nature of the grievance, you have the right to be accompanied.

Once you have exhausted your employer's procedures and you are still not satisfied, you may be able to go to an Employment Tribunal or the civil courts. You would normally have to show that your employer had denied you your legal rights or was in breach of your contract of employment, including the implied duties discussed earlier in this chapter.

If you cannot show this, there is little more that you can do, unless you are in a unionized workplace and your union is able to take the matter up as being one of more general concern to all the staff.

The right to be accompanied

All workers have the right to be accompanied at a disciplinary or grievance hearing. This right applies to all workers, not only to employees, so it does not matter whether or not you have a contract of employment with your employer or hiring company. You have the right to be accompanied by a trade union officer or representative, or a fellow worker. You do not have the right to bring in a lawyer or other adviser. Union officers and representatives will have been trained and accredited to accompany workers. They are likely to bring valuable experience to any formal proceedings. They can accompany you even if the union is not 'recognized'.

If a union is recognized by your employer (see Chapter 1) it is very likely that there will be an agreed disciplinary and grievance procedure and the union will have full representation rights in relation to its members. This is one of the normal benefits of union recognition, and in some workplaces there are employer–union agreements on disciplinary and grievance issues even where there are no negotiations on pay and conditions.

The legal right to be accompanied at a disciplinary hearing is triggered if the hearing could result in a formal warning, confirmation of a previous formal warning or some other action such as suspension, demotion or dismissal. It is, therefore, widely drawn and it is hard to see how your representative could be excluded from any formal hearing. However, the right to be accompanied does not apply to a more informal conversation with your manager about your conduct, though if you think a discussion that starts out informally has become formal you should say so and ask for it to be resumed with your representative present and under proper procedures. On the other hand, it may be best to keep things informal, as this prevents formal action being taken against you.

With grievance hearings, the right to be accompanied only applies if your complaint concerns a legal duty owed to you by your employer, for example, your employer's obligation to ensure that you are not bullied or harassed. In practice it should be possible to argue that any likely grievance may have a bearing on a legal duty, and it is unlikely that any but the most grudging or anti-union employer will try to differentiate between legal and non-legal grievances, although they may screen complaints that they consider to be trivial.

If your employer does not inform you that you may bring a trade union representative or a fellow worker to a hearing, or tries to prevent you from exercising your right, you can make a 'reasonable' request to your employer to be accompanied. If they continue to refuse, you can make a complaint to an Employment Tribunal. 'Reasonable' in this context means that the hearing complies with the conditions above and you make the request as soon as possible after being notified of the hearing. It is a flexible term, though, and if you have special circumstances – for example, you do not speak English as a first language and need a helper at the hearing – it would be 'reasonable' to request to be accompanied.

6

Discrimination

The principles behind the law on discrimination are easy to state. In practice, however, this is a complicated area of law.

Even though some anti-discrimination law has been on the statute books for more than 30 years, there is still some way to go. Women, on average, earn less than men, and black people earn less than white people. Despite some progress, people in positions of authority at the top of organizations, and even in middle management and supervisor roles, are more likely to be white and male.

It is more than 10 years since disability discrimination laws were introduced, yet disabled people face considerable barriers to getting good jobs.

Laws protecting against discrimination on the basis of age, sexual orientation and religion or belief are more recent.

What the law says

You have the right not to be discriminated against at work on the grounds of your sex, race, disability, religion, belief, sexual orientation or age. A separate law, the Equal Pay Act, also provides for equal pay between men and women. This chapter outlines your basic rights, but this is one of the most complex areas of employment law. If you run into problems you should always consult your union representative or a legal or other specialist adviser.

The good news is that discrimination laws apply to almost everyone at work. They cover you when you apply for a job and from the first day of your job. It does not matter whether you are an employee, a worker, self-employed or a trainee.

If the discrimination happens while you are at work or while you are working for your employer, your employer is liable, even if it is not the employer personally who is discriminating against you.

There are useful special questionnaire procedures in discrimination law that mean you can ask your employer for further information if you think you have a case against them. Ask your union representative or adviser about these procedures.

If you think you have been discriminated against unlawfully, you can take a case to an Employment Tribunal, but you must do this within three months of the incident you are complaining about. You might be awarded compensation and damages. This award can include an element to cover injury to your feelings. There is no upper limit on the amount that can be awarded in discrimination claims, and some large awards have hit the headlines. However, these large awards are the exception, not the rule.

What is discrimination?

Most of our discrimination laws share a common approach and similar definitions. The law generally prohibits four kinds of action. These are direct discrimination, indirect discrimination, harassment and victimization.

Direct discrimination

People directly discriminate against you if they treat you less favourably than they would treat someone else because of your sex, race, disability, age, sexual orientation, or religion or belief. Examples of direct discrimination might include a case where a male employee is offered training but it is refused to a woman 'because she might go off and have a baby', or where a well-qualified black person applies for a job and is told it has gone – and then a white person applies and is offered an interview.

You should note that direct discrimination on the grounds of disability requires you to show that you were treated less favourably than a non-disabled person who has the same abilities as you. 'Disability-related discrimination', which is a different form of discrimination prohibited by the Disability Discrimination Act, is more common. It occurs when an employer fails to make an adjustment to working practices or workplace equipment in order to accommodate someone with a disability where it is reasonable to do so.

If a tribunal rules that you have been treated in a directly discriminatory way then the employer's motive for their actions does not affect the outcome of the case and they cannot avoid an unlawful ruling by trying to justify their treatment of you (except in the case of age discrimination). For example, if a gay barman is hired for a pub but the landlord later sacks him because some customers complain and say they will not drink there unless he goes, the landlord is guilty of discrimination even if he says that he personally did not want the barman to go but was forced into taking the action by his customers. Similarly, it would be unlawful sex discrimination if an employer refused to employ a woman in an all-male workplace because he was worried she might have problems fitting in and could be bullied or sexually harassed. Even where employers don't realize they are discriminating, the unfavourable treatment is still unlawful.

Indirect discrimination

Indirect discrimination is a harder concept to pin down. It happens when an employer establishes a 'provision, criterion or practice' that puts people of a certain sex, race, sexual orientation, age, or religion or belief at a particular disadvantage when compared to others. (Note that indirect discrimination does not apply to disability.) Employers may be able to avoid a ruling against them if they can show that the provision, criterion or practice was a proportionate way of them achieving a legitimate business goal. However, if there is an obvious, less discriminatory way of them achieving the same goal it will be hard for them to justify the provision, criterion or practice and it could be ruled unlawful.

The following examples show how indirect discrimination can happen:

■ A bus company's recruitment literature says its drivers must have a high level of fluency in English in order to drive a bus with a conductor. But it may be hard for it to justify the need for such strong language skills, as the conductor will be dealing with all the passengers. Therefore the requirement could be unlawful race discrimination because it puts people of different national or ethnic origins at a disadvantage. On the other hand, if the company was recruiting for a one-person bus and the driver had to collect fares and help passengers then the company could legitimately require higher standards of English.

■ A shop decides to open seven days a week and draws up a roster that means some Sunday working for all employees. One worker is a devout Christian and objects to working on Sundays. The employer refuses to listen to her objections and insists that all employees must work on Sundays. She decides she has no choice but to resign. She may be able to successfully claim indirect religious discrimination, and her case would be strengthened by the fact that the employer did not consider any alternatives – for example, there may have been others within the workforce who wanted to work more Sundays and would have swapped shifts with her.

■ A firm operates a 'last in, first out' (LIFO) redundancy policy. As older workers are likely to have longer service than younger workers, this policy is indirectly discriminatory against younger workers. It could therefore be unlawful, particularly if LIFO is the only criterion used to select people for redundancy. However, if it is one of a wide range of factors that are taken into consideration the employer may be justified in using it.

Indirect discrimination cases are very tricky. You have to show that people of your sex, race, age, etc have been put at a particular disadvantage and that the provision, criterion or practice in question has actually harmed you. You will also need to be prepared to show that such a provision, criterion or practice was not justified and that there was another less discriminatory way of the employer achieving the same goal.

However, in any legal case about discrimination, if you can show some initial facts that suggest your employer has discriminated against you, it is then up to your employer to prove that they haven't. Also, if you work for a public sector employer, your employer is under extra legal duties to prevent unlawful discrimination and promote equality of opportunity on the grounds of race, sex and disability. This means they should be monitoring the workforce, assessing the impact of their policies on different groups, and publishing written equality action plans. Further information about these public sector duties can be gained from the Equality and Human Rights Commission or from your union representative.

Harassment

Discrimination laws protect you from harassment linked to your sex, race, disability, age, religion/belief or sexual orientation. Harassment is commonly defined as behaviour that violates your dignity or creates an intimidating, hostile, degrading, humiliating or offensive environment for you. The person who is harassing you may claim that he or she was just joking or that it was just 'firm management'. But you don't have to prove that the person intended to harass you. If you found his

or her behaviour offensive or degrading, it is sufficient for you
to show that it had that effect on you. If you make a legal
claim, a tribunal will objectively assess what the effect of the
person's behaviour was and they will particularly consider your
perception of it.

If you are being harassed it is important to make it clear to
the harasser that you find his or her behaviour offensive. If
possible, you should ask the harasser to stop and inform your
employer. Remember, your employer has a duty to protect you
from such treatment, and they are liable if they do not take
action to prevent it. Also tell your union representative or other
adviser and keep evidence of the harasser's behaviour, perhaps
in a diary, and try to get witnesses.

It's the pattern that counts

Kate White was fed up with the constant stream of sexual innu-
endo she faced every day at work. Even in an interview with her
boss when she was trying to be promoted, he had told her that
she would do better with a low-cut dress. Eventually she
decided to take action and took a case to a tribunal claiming
sex discrimination. Although the tribunal agreed that 58 different incidents of sexual harassment took place, her boss
claimed that it was all light-hearted and jokey, and that he
commonly made similar remarks to his male colleagues.

The tribunal dismissed her case, on the grounds that none of
the 58 incidents were serious enough to count as discriminatory. But she won an appeal. The Employment Appeal Tribunal
said the pattern of behaviour should be looked at as a whole
and made clear that there is a difference between jokes
between male staff and remarks made by a man to a woman.

Victimization

Victimization occurs when someone is treated unfavourably
after complaining about or alleging discrimination or harass-

ment. It includes actions taken against you after you have left employment, such as a refusal by your former employer to give you a reference. The law also protects you from victimization if you have helped someone else bring a complaint – for example, if you gave evidence on behalf of a colleague in a discrimination case.

Exceptions to discrimination law

There are two common exceptions to discrimination law. The first is 'positive action'. This allows employers to encourage people from groups that are under-represented to apply for jobs. They can also target skills training at under-represented groups to enable them to apply. However, recruitment decisions must still be based on individual merit.

The second exception is where there is a 'genuine occupational requirement' for the job-holder to be of a particular race, sex, age, etc. This will generally only apply to a very small number of situations – for example, where an actor is required to play a character who is a woman or who is black. However, within the religious and sexual orientation discrimination laws there are additional exceptions that allow religious organizations to require someone to be of a particular faith or sexual orientation.

Sex

The Sex Discrimination Act means that you cannot be treated less favourably because of your gender. It also specifically protects women from being treated unfavourably because they are pregnant or on maternity leave. And it prohibits discrimination based on the fact that someone is intending to undergo or has undergone gender reassignment.

Because women are more likely to be carers and to work part-time the protection from sex discrimination often overlaps with other areas of employment law. For example, if a woman has a request for flexible working turned down, this could be indirect sex discrimination, as a refusal to allow flexible working practices will put more women than men at a disadvantage. Similarly, if you are a woman working part-time and you are being treated less favourably than full-timers you might have a sex discrimination claim as well as a claim under the Part-Time Worker Regulations.

It is also important to note that, if you are being paid less or are receiving lower contractual terms and conditions than someone of the opposite sex who is doing similar work, then this is not covered by the Sex Discrimination Act but is instead covered by the Equal Pay Act, which is explained later in this chapter.

Race

The Race Relations Act protects people from discrimination based on their race, national or ethnic origins, colour or nationality. It also protects you if you are discriminated against because someone thinks you belong to a particular racial group or if you associate with someone of a different racial group – for example, if you are married to someone of a different ethnic background – and you are harassed at work because of this relationship.

Disability

The Disability Discrimination Act 1995 (DDA) gives disabled workers some protections against discrimination at work. It prohibits discrimination against disabled job applicants, employees and contractors. It applies to recruitment, promotion, employee benefits, disciplinary proceedings, dismissal, harassment and victimization.

To be covered by the DDA you must have an impairment or medical condition that makes it substantially difficult for you to carry out normal day to day activities. These are defined as mobility, manual dexterity, coordination, continence, ability to lift everyday objects, speech, hearing, eyesight, memory, ability to concentrate and learn and awareness of danger. The impairment or condition must be long term, which is defined as lasting at least 12 months.

A wide range of conditions are covered, for example:

■ conditions that have a slight effect on day-to-day activities, but which are expected to become substantial, for example, arthritis, cancer, multiple sclerosis;
■ conditions that would have a serious effect if not controlled by medication such as severe depression, or by aids such as, for instance, artificial limbs;
■ conditions that fluctuate such as ME; and
■ severe disfigurements.

The DDA covers mental illnesses, but people with mental illnesses can find it difficult to establish that they are covered by the Act.

To be covered by the Act, all disabled people have to show that their condition has a substantial and long-term negative effect on their ability to carry out 'normal day-to-day activities'.

One difficulty with the legal definition of 'day-to-day activities' is that it does not include working in a job. You are unlikely to be covered by the DDA if you have a mental illness that only affects your ability to do your job, even though that is precisely the situation that some people with a mental illness triggered by stress at work find themselves in.

Discrimination involves the employer treating a disabled person less favourably than a non-disabled person would be treated. The difference in treatment must be related to the person's disability. For example, a person might be dismissed because their hearing deteriorates to the point where they can no longer answer the telephone. This would be discrimination unless the employer can justify their actions. For example, the employer might say that it was necessary for that employee to be able to answer the telephone. But the employer is expected to make 'reasonable adjustments' to solve the problem. In this case the employer could install a minicom or adjust the person's duties.

The idea of the 'reasonable adjustments' is to remove obstacles that place the disabled person at a disadvantage. Examples could be altering premises, changing working hours, allowing time off for treatment, buying new equipment, supplying additional training or even just providing a reserved parking space. What is 'reasonable' depends on the individual case, but you have to take into account how effective the adjustment will be, the cost and the employer's resources. Clearly an employer cannot be expected to make adjustments unless they have been informed of your disability and needs.

As with sex and race discrimination legislation, the DDA makes it unlawful for an employer to victimize a person for alleging disability discrimination, bringing a case or giving evidence in a case. This applies whether or not the victimized person is disabled.

The law on disability discrimination is complicated and you should not embark on a case without taking specialist advice. You can take a case to an Employment Tribunal, and claims have to be made within three months of the discrimination you are complaining about. The tribunal can award compensation, including for injury to feelings. There is no upper limit on compensation. The tribunal may also recommend that the employer makes adjustments in the workplace.

Sexual orientation

The situation where there was no specific protection in law for people unfairly treated because of their sexual orientation came to an end on 1 December 2003, when the Employment

Equality (Sexual Orientation) Regulations 2003 came into force. Since that date, employees have been able to go to an employment tribunal in the same way as if they are claiming discrimination on other existing grounds.

The rights cover recruitment and dismissal, harassment, access to training or promotion, victimization, access to employee benefits available to other workers, and indirect discrimination.

The main exception in the rules is where the employment is 'for the purposes of organized religion'. The government say they intend that this should be very narrowly applied so that it would be restricted to ministers of religion and similar jobs. But unions and gay rights campaigners are worried that it will be applied more broadly to cover wider groups of employees of religious organizations, for example teachers and other staff in church schools. This is likely to be an area of considerable legal controversy. It is possible that the government may be challenged in Europe on the grounds that they have not fully met the provisions of the European Directive. On the other hand, some religious employers with reactionary views on gay rights are likely to resist any legal challenges to them by staff.

Religion or belief

The Religion or Belief Regulations were introduced at the same time as the Sexual Orientation Regulations. They do not define what a religion or belief is, so a key question is: what kinds of beliefs are protected by the law? The government intention was that philosophical beliefs similar to religious beliefs should be covered. So courts and tribunals will consider things like whether or not there is collective worship or a clear system of beliefs that profoundly affects and determines how you live your life. In addition to well-recognized religions, other beliefs such as paganism will be covered. The regulations also protect people who do not have religious belief from discrimination, such as atheists or agnostics.

There are specific exceptions within the law that mean that religious or faith-based organizations can require that you share their religious beliefs in order to be employed by them. However, these exceptions are not as wide as you might think and they do not apply to all jobs within such organizations. For example, it will probably be lawful for a faith-based school recruiting a pastoral care teacher to require applicants to belong to the religion if the job involves giving spiritual guidance on a regular basis. But it would be difficult for the faith-based school to insist that its maths teacher or school receptionist share the same religious ethos.

Age

Regulations outlawing age discrimination took effect on 1 October 2006. They protect all workers from discrimination on grounds of age – not just older workers. For example, if you've been denied a promotion because you are 'too young' or refused access to development training because you don't have as many years of employment ahead of you as younger colleagues, you may have a claim. You will also be protected from discrimination based on your perceived age – for example, if someone says you look too young or too old for a job.

Traditionally, there have been many age-based rules in the workplace, and so the Age Regulations could potentially have a big impact. But age discrimination protection is different from the other laws because it allows employers to justify direct discrimination if they can show it is a proportionate way of them achieving a legitimate business goal. For example, an employer may decide that for health and safety reasons they do not want to employ someone in a job that involves operating dangerous machinery because of the person's age. The employer would have to make sure though that their decision was based on an objective assessment of the actual risk, rather than just being based on stereotypical assumptions about younger or older workers.

The law also specifically permits some age-related policies or practices. For example, service-related pay and benefits that are based on service up to five years are allowed. So are age-based rates of pay that mirror the national minimum wage, the age-based bands in the statutory redundancy pay scheme, and age-related rules and benefits in occupational pension schemes.

Retirement

Employers can no longer force you to retire below age 65 unless they can objectively justify setting a lower retirement age, which will be difficult in most cases. You can still voluntarily retire at an age below 65 and receive an occupational pension from age 50 if your scheme allows it (this will increase to 55 in 2010).

However, if you are aged 65 or older, your employer can retire you by following the statutory retirement procedure, which is set out in the Age Regulations. This is a complicated procedure, and it is important that you seek further advice from your union representative or ACAS, especially if you are being retired against your wishes and want to challenge the decision. (At the time of writing, a case is pending in the European Court of Justice that may give you more protection against forced retirement.)

Your employer begins the procedure by writing to you six to 12 months in advance of the intended date of retirement. If you do not want to retire you can request to stay on either indefinitely or for a fixed period of time. Your request must be in writing and be given to your employer three to six months before the intended date of retirement. Your employer has a duty to consider your request and should organize a meeting to discuss it with you. If they refuse your request you have the right to appeal against the decision. This may be difficult, as your employer is not obliged to tell you why they turned your request down – although it is good practice for them to inform you of their reasons.

If your employer correctly follows the procedure and retires you on the intended date of retirement then it will be difficult to challenge the decision. However, if they do not follow the procedure it will not necessarily be a retirement and you might be able to bring claims of unfair dismissal and age discrimination. You should seek advice before going down this route.

Equal pay

EU and UK laws give women and men the right to equal pay. Under the Equal Pay Act a woman can claim equal pay with a man who is doing:

■ 'like work' (that is, work that is the same or broadly similar); or
■ 'work rated equivalent' under a job evaluation study; or
■ 'work of equal value'.

The Act covers workers – including apprentices and people working from home – whether on full-time, part-time, casual or temporary contracts. It doesn't matter how long you have worked for your employer. It also covers you if you have a contract to carry work out personally for someone else.

If you are a woman taking an equal pay claim you have to compare your pay with that of a specific man. Your first step, therefore, is to find a suitable man who will be known as the 'comparator'. He does not have to agree to this. This can be difficult as, particularly in workplaces where there tend to be individual salary packages rather than groups all doing the same job, it can be hard to find out how much other people earn. And it's not quite polite to ask! However, you can submit an equal pay questionnaire to your employer. This can be downloaded from the government's Women and Equality Unit website.

Not everyone can be a comparator. The law says the comparator has to be 'in the same employment'. Clearly, anyone who works with you and has the same employer can be a comparator. But it can be stretched more widely than this. You can also choose a comparator who works 'at the same establishment' for an associated employer. If this is not possible, you can also look for a comparator at another workplace if the place of work meets two conditions. Firstly, it must belong to your employer (or to an associated employer). Secondly, people must be working on the same terms and conditions. In the public sector this can give quite a wide scope for comparison, but it can be tougher in the private sector, particularly in a small business.

How far you can look for a comparator is one of those complex areas of law where it is very hard to give general guidance. Many cases will depend on precisely this point, and different courts and tribunals have interpreted the law in different ways. Also, EU law lets you make wider comparisons than UK law. This is an area where it is crucial to get expert advice.

Once you have found your comparator there are three ways you can establish you are not getting equal pay.

The first is the most straightforward test. You have to show your comparator is doing 'the same or broadly similar work'. This does not mean you have to be doing identical jobs. They can count as broadly similar as long as any differences between them are not of 'practical importance'. A difference of 'practical importance' could include extra responsibility or additional duties.

The second way you can claim equal pay is by showing that your comparator is doing work that has been 'rated as equivalent under a job evaluation scheme'. This is the kind of scheme that employers often use to set their pay structures.

Normally, outside experts with experience of this work and a wide knowledge of how different organizations relate pay to different jobs will carry out the evaluation. They will look at all the different jobs and rate them by different criteria such as the responsibilities involved, the skills required and the knowledge needed. You will probably end up with scores of some kind for each job.

You cannot make your employer carry out a job evaluation exercise in order to make an equal pay claim. But if they have done one and accepted its results then you can bring a claim using this as your evidence.

The job evaluation scheme must also meet certain tests. The court will need to know that it was thorough, with proper tools used to measure each job. It cannot just be a rough ranking of jobs drawn up on the back of an envelope.

The third way of claiming equal pay is by showing that your work is of **equal value** to that done by a man in the same employment, even though his job is different. In some ways you can think of this as a do-it-yourself job evaluation scheme. You have to show that your work is equal in value to that done by your comparator, using the same kind of headings such as effort, skill and decision-making that a job evaluation study would use.

But claiming equal pay for work of equal value is more complicated than showing that you are doing 'like work' or work rated as equivalent under a job evaluation scheme. Again, you have to find your 'equal value' comparator. He must successfully meet the 'in the same employment' test requirements as a comparator who is doing the same job as you. But you can look much wider, as you need to find a man paid more than you but whose job has the same value even if it is completely different.

Successful 'equal value' comparisons have been made between:

■ a woman canteen worker and a male shipyard worker;
■ women fish packers with a general labourer;
■ nursery nurses with a waste technician and architectural technician; and
■ a speech therapist with senior pharmacist and a senior clinical psychologist.

The tribunal procedure for claiming equal pay for work of equal value is more complicated than in other equal pay cases. You should not even think of taking an equal value case without seeking expert advice. You should also bear in mind that you can take an equal pay case to a tribunal only while you are still employed or within six months after the end of employment, unless certain exceptions apply, such as where your employer has deliberately concealed an important fact relating to your case. You will need expert advice in these circumstances.

Part-time work

Part-time work is not defined in law. It is generally taken to mean any hours below the normal full-time hours where you work. Part-time workers have some protection in law against discrimination, both under the Sex Discrimination Act and under regulations introduced in 2000, as we explain below.

Part-time workers and sex discrimination and equal pay laws

The Sex Discrimination Act 1975 and the Equal Pay Act 1970 do not mention part-time workers. But most part-time workers are women, and discrimination against part-time workers can often be indirect sex discrimination (we explain earlier in this chapter how to spot indirect discrimination). Excluding part-time workers from pay-related benefits, or paying them lower hourly rates, can in some circumstances be indirect pay discrimination.

There have been some successful cases – but indirect discrimination is always more difficult to show than direct. You have to show that the employer is imposing a 'condition or requirement' that affects considerably more women than men.

For example, your employer might have a rule saying that only full-time workers can get contractual sick pay. If most of the men in your workplace work full-time, and most of the women part-time, that could be indirect discrimination unless the employer can justify the rule. But your claim could fail, for example, if you work for an employer where there are no or very few men and most of the women employees are full-time. In a case like that you could not show that more women than men are adversely affected by the employer's rule.

Other examples of possible indirect sex discrimination claims might be where:

■ Your employer excludes part-time workers from benefits like private health insurance or a profit-related bonus scheme. If where you work, most of the men work full-time and most of the women work part-time, more women than men would be excluded, so a claim might succeed. Or if full-time workers get extra annual leave after one year's service, while part-time workers have to work for two years before getting more holiday. Again, if most of the full-time workers are men, and most of the part-time workers women, you could have a case.

Another way some women have successfully used the indirect discrimination provisions is by arguing that they should be able to come back to work after maternity leave on reduced hours. The argument is that more women than men find it difficult to work full-time, because more women than men take responsibility for young children.

But although some cases have been won on this basis, others have not. There is a clear case for a change in the law to give stronger rights, as this indirect discrimination route is very uncertain. You should not think of trying this route without taking specialist advice. In the meantime, there are new rights for parents to make requests for flexible working (see Chapter 4).

Part-time work regulations

These regulations should make it easier for part-time workers to claim equality with full-time workers without having to enter the minefield of indirect sex discrimination. The regulations do not give you the right to work part-time – so if you are a woman wanting to work reduced hours because of your caring responsibilities, the legal routes open to you would be using indirect discrimination arguments or under the right for parents to request flexible working.

The regulations are designed so that part-time workers are not treated as second class when it comes to pay and non-wage benefits. In order to bring a case you need to show that you are being treated less favourably than a full-time worker who the law accepts as a valid comparator, and this is because of your part-time status. Most workers are covered. It does not matter whether you are temporary or full-time, an employee or a worker. The right starts from your first day at work. As long as there are workers doing a similar job, working longer hours than you, and getting better treatment, then you can bring a case.

While only employees can claim unfair dismissal if they are sacked for making a claim, everyone is protected against what the law calls *detriment* – such as being passed over for promotion – because you have claimed your rights or helped a colleague to claim under this law.

The regulations are broad in their scope and almost any term or condition is covered including:

■ overtime pay (once the part-time employee has worked more than the normal full-time hours);
■ contractual sick pay;
■ access to any occupational pension scheme;
■ training;
■ holidays;
■ maternity leave, pay and parental leave;
■ access to career break schemes.

With whom can you compare yourself?

To be able to claim your rights under the new law you have to show that your treatment has been less favourable than that of a full-time worker. But you cannot compare yourself with just any worker.

It has to be:

■ a full-time worker, working for the same employer, in your own workplace;
■ working under the same type of contract as you; and
■ doing the same or similar work to yours.

If there is no full-time worker at your workplace who matches this description, you can choose someone from another of your employer's locations.

If you have been working full-time and shift to part-time work you can also compare your treatment with that which you previously enjoyed when you were full-time. For example, if you have taken maternity leave and it is agreed that you return to the same job but part-time, you should be able to keep your existing terms and conditions, pro-rata to your working hours, unless your employer can justify the difference. You have this right to compare your situation to the one before you went on maternity leave provided you were not off for more than 12 months.

As long as there are full-time workers in your workplace doing generally the same work, you will be covered. If not, you will also be able to compare yourself with full-time workers at another location, provided they have the same employer as you and are doing broadly similar work to yours.

But it is important to note that your full-time comparator must generally have the same type of contract as you. This means, for example, that if you are part-time and employed as an apprentice, you cannot compare yourself to a full-time employee who is not an apprentice. However, you may still be able to compare yourself to a permanent full-timer even if you only have a fixed-term contract. You will need further advice on this.

Writing to your employer

Once you have found the eligible full-time worker (your comparator) who is being treated better than you, you should write to your employer and ask why you are being treated differently. Before you do this, however, you should talk it through with an adviser, from your union if possible.

Once your employer has your letter, they have to reply within 21 days. If they do not, a tribunal can take this as evidence that your rights have been breached.

You will need to discuss their reply with your union or other adviser, to see if an Employment Tribunal is likely to accept your employer's arguments or side with you.

There are also similar rights for temporary workers not to be discriminated against in comparison with permanent workers. If you are a temporary worker suffering discrimination, contact your union representative or a legal or other specialist adviser.

7

Getting the sack

Dismissal

About the worst thing that can happen to you at work is losing your job. The legal term for getting the sack is dismissal. Your employer will tell you that you are no longer wanted, and that from a certain date your employment will come to an end. At the end of this chapter you will find the dismissal maze. This is a table that will help you through the concepts in this chapter.

A dismissal can take place in a number of ways:

- Your employer can terminate your contract.
- Your job can be made redundant.
- Your employer can decide not to renew a fixed-term contract.
- Your employer can claim that you have dismissed yourself by your actions – either misconduct by you or your inability to do the job competently.
- Or, in some circumstances, you can leave and claim that you were 'constructively dismissed'.

Notice

Your contract will normally say what notice your employer is required to give you if they intend to dismiss you. It will also normally say what notice you must give if you want to leave your job. But the law does set out minimum standards for periods of notice and your contract must not give you any less than the following. Your employer must give you at least one week's notice after one month's employment, two weeks' notice after two years' employment, three weeks after three years, and so on up to 12 weeks after 12 years or more. Most employees are entitled to receive payment during this statutory notice period. If you are not given adequate notice of dismissal, you can sue the employer for 'wrongful dismissal' in a court or tribunal (see below and Chapter 8).

Once you have had your job for more than a month you must give at least one week's notice. This does not increase. However, your contract can set out a longer notice period for you to give to your employer.

Employers and employees can waive their right to notice or agree to a payment instead of receiving a period of notice (often called a 'payment in lieu of notice'). The law only allows such a payment if you agree to it or if it is allowed by terms in your contract. If your employer is keen for you to leave immediately, you may be able to use this to increase the payment you are given.

Either you or your employer can terminate the contract of employment without notice if the conduct of the other justifies it. You should only walk out if you believe that your employer is acting so badly that you can make a successful claim for constructive dismissal (see below). Although you may be so desperate that you just want to quit on the spot, you should, if possible, take advice as to whether you have a good case. If you do walk out, your employer may deduct a week's wages from what is owing to you as you have not given notice. You would have to win a constructive dismissal case to get this back.

If your employer sacks you without notice, it has to be for a substantial reason. If, for example, you have been found guilty of gross misconduct, such as violence in the workplace, race discrimination or theft, then your employer is very likely to ask you to leave the premises immediately. Most contracts of employment will specify circumstances under which the employer may dismiss the employee without giving notice.

Written statement of reasons for dismissal

Once you have held your job for a year, your employer must give you a written statement of why you have been dismissed if you ask for it. The law says this must be given in response to either a written or verbal request, but it is always a good idea to put any communication with your employer about issues such as this in writing and keep a copy. The employer must provide this 'written statement for reasons of dismissal' – its legal name – within 14 days of your request.

If you get the sack while you are pregnant or on maternity leave then you should be given a written statement automatically. You should not have to ask for it and you should get one, however long you have worked for your employer. If you do not get one, you will have a very strong tribunal case.

Constructive dismissal

A constructive dismissal is one where your circumstances become so difficult for you that you are convinced that you have no alternative but to leave. This can occur, for example, if your employer makes major changes to your contract, or your job, without your consent and you find the changes unacceptable. You must exercise great caution in resigning in this way as it is extremely difficult to satisfy a court or tribunal that the circumstances made it impossible for you to continue. Even if you do convince the court, you will probably not get your old job back but will get compensation – though this may not be very much – instead.

Wrongful dismissal

A wrongful dismissal is a dismissal that is in breach of your contract of employment, or goes against something provided for in your contract. It is not the same as an unfair dismissal, which is explained below.

Wrongful dismissals can include:

■ a dismissal without proper notice;
■ failure to pay your wages in full during the notice period; or
■ any other breach of the provisions in your contract about notice.

As a claim for wrongful dismissal is a breach of contract claim, you can pursue your complaint in either the civil courts or an Employment Tribunal. The advantages of the court route are that damages are unlimited if you make your claim in the High Court (or Court of Session in Scotland). You can also make a claim in a county court (or sheriff's court in Scotland) if you are claiming less than £25,000.

This is the same upper limit as in an Employment Tribunal, but a claim for wrongful dismissal to an Employment Tribunal must be made within three calendar months of the dismissal occurring. For the civil courts there is a six-year period following the dismissal during which you can make a claim (five years in Scotland).

The disadvantages of using the civil courts are that you will need legal representation and the costs of losing could be high, if your former employer's costs are awarded against you. Employment Tribunals are more informal, and costs awards are less likely to be made. You should take detailed advice about the best way to pursue a wrongful dismissal claim. It is hard to generalize, but it is likely that only high earners are likely to be advised to take the riskier, though potentially more rewarding, route of a claim in the civil courts.

Unfair dismissal

If you are unfairly dismissed you can take a case against your employer. If you have been dismissed and have also been discriminated against on the basis of sex, race, disability or trade union membership you can claim discrimination *and* unfair dismissal, which may result in higher compensation.

To work out whether you have been dismissed unfairly, it is easiest to explain what the law considers a fair dismissal. If you have not been dismissed fairly then you must have been unfairly dismissed.

Other than in some special cases set out on pages 166–67 in the section on qualifying conditions, you must have worked for your employer for more than a year to gain protection against unfair dismissal. You must also normally get your claim in within three calendar months of getting the sack.

Fair dismissal

A fair dismissal is one that takes place for the following reasons:

■ your conduct;
■ your capability or qualifications for the job;
■ redundancy (your job is no longer needed);
■ a legal requirement that prevents the employment being continued;
■ some other substantial reason that could justify the dismissal;
■ retirement.

Conduct

Conduct covers your behaviour both on and, in some cases, off the job. For a dismissal on grounds of conduct to be considered fair, your employer would generally need to be able to show that they have conducted a proper investigation into your alleged misconduct and given you a chance to answer the case in a properly convened disciplinary hearing. The Employment Relations Act 1999 gave everyone involved in a disciplinary or grievance hearing the right to be accompanied by a fellow employee or a trade union representative, even if the employer does not recognize the union (see Chapter 5).

Some allowance is made for small businesses when considering the procedures used, as tribunals will expect higher standards from companies with full-time personnel officers. But small firms will still need to be able to show that they have established the facts of the case and given you a chance to respond, with representation if you wish, and to have a hearing, in line with the minimum statutory procedures.

Your misconduct must also be sufficiently bad to justify dismissal. Misconduct outside the workplace can be grounds for a fair dismissal. For example, it is likely that a tribunal would find dismissal of someone employed as a driver for a driving-related offence in his or her own car to be fair, but not the dismissal of someone who does not drive as part of his or her job. In other words, dismissal for an off-the-job offence must be shown to relate in some way to your job.

Clocking out for good

Frank Jones had worked for a biscuit firm for 22 years. He was sacked for clocking in for a workmate, who had slipped back to the cloakroom to collect a cap that he had forgotten but which he had to wear for work. The employees' handbook listed clocking in offences as among those regarded by the company as 'breaches of regulations [that] will result in instant dismissal'. There was also a notice above the clock that said 'It is a serious offence to stamp another employee's time card. Any irregularities on the card must be reported immediately. Failure to do so means instant dismissal.' The last two words were written in large letters. Frank was seen falsifying the clock by witnesses and admitted to it.

Frank claimed unfair dismissal. His argument at the tribunal was that dismissal was too draconian a penalty after 22 years' service, and that a warning would have been more appropriate. But he lost. The tribunal decided that the dismissal was fair as all staff had been given plenty of notice that a clocking in offence would result in dismissal.

Tribunals have generally treated clocking in offences with great severity. They have, on the whole, accepted employer arguments, reflected in many works rules, that clocking offences warrant instant dismissal. On the other hand, you may have a case if you can show that other workers were treated differently after committing the same offence, or that fiddling clock cards has been a common practice which everyone has previously ignored.

More people succeed in Employment Tribunal cases by showing that their employer has failed to carry out fair procedures than by getting a tribunal to agree that their employer has over-reacted to misconduct. This is because the legal test they apply is whether a *reasonable employer* would dismiss a member of staff on these grounds. This is not the same as asking whether the misconduct is serious enough to justify dismissal, but whether other employers would do the same.

See Chapter 8 for more about Employment Tribunals and their procedures.

The pub lunch

Sid French worked on a passenger ferry. During one of his shifts he went to a pub to have lunch. He was joined by two workmates. The employers had a strict rule that employees should not enter licensed premises while working. A manager went to the pub and immediately suspended all three employees. There was no suggestion that Mr French was drunk – he had merely gone to the most convenient place to obtain food – but his two colleagues acted in a way consistent with their being drunk. On the following day all three were summarily dismissed.

Management argued that as all three had broken the same rule, all three must be punished equally. But Sid claimed unfair dismissal and won.

The tribunal took the view that there were enough differences between the conduct of Mr French and that of his colleagues to make a reasonable employer distinguish between them. To treat all employees the same as a matter of course, without considering the particular circumstances of each individual, simply should not be done.

Many employers try to argue that there are some offences that warrant automatic penalties – no excuse being accepted. This case reinforces the argument that each individual case needs to be considered, and you should have the right to present your case in a disciplinary hearing.

Capability

The second ground for fair dismissal is capability. For the first year of your job you do not have any protection against unfair dismissal (except in the limited circumstances set out on pages 166–67), so your employer can sack you easily if they do not think you are up to the job for the first 12 months you work for them. Once you have worked for more than a year, your employer will need to be able to show that they have followed proper procedures that establish that you cannot perform your job competently.

The most common reason for a fair dismissal in these circumstances is when your health deteriorates to the point that you cannot do your job any longer. However, your employer would need to show that they could not make changes in your working environment that would allow you to continue to work. The Disability Discrimination Act may be relevant in some cases (see Chapter 6).

Your employer will still have to follow the disciplinary procedure, informing you that your job is at risk, and having a hearing where you have the right to be accompanied, so that you can make representations.

Redundancy

You are made redundant if your job is ended. Legally, it is the job that is made redundant, not the worker. This is a complex area covered in more detail on pages 169–70. If you are one of a group of workers doing more or less the same job and only some of you have been selected for redundancy then your employer must be able to show that the workers to be made redundant have been chosen fairly.

Dismissal on the grounds of redundancy will be deemed unfair if the employee is selected for redundancy, when others in the same circumstances are not, on grounds of:

■ trade union membership or activities;
■ taking certain types of action in relation to health and safety – for example, refusing to do a job where the employee is convinced that there is a serious risk to his or her health and safety;
■ any reason in connection with maternity;
■ asserting a statutory right – for example, asking to be paid the minimum wage;
■ refusing to do shop or betting work on Sundays (see Chapter 5);
■ acting as an employees' representative in relation to consultation on redundancies or a business transfer;
■ performing any duties relating to an employee's role as an occupational pension fund trustee.

Dismissal on the grounds of redundancy may also be unfair if your employer has not given you adequate warning of it or if they have failed to consider offering you another job.

Legal requirement

A typical example of this would be getting the sack from a job as a driver because you have lost your licence. However, your employer must also show there is no alternative employment with the company.

Some other substantial reason

This fifth basis for a fair dismissal causes real difficulties as the phrasing is vague. Tribunals have devised various tests that they use when they come to consider whether or not a dismissal was for a 'substantial' reason. But at the end of the day the tribunal has to make a judgement as to whether or not the facts of the matter justified the action of the employer. It will consider whether or not any grievance or disciplinary procedures were properly used. In these circumstances, it is particularly important for employees to ensure that they have the statutory written reasons for dismissal, as described above.

Retirement

If you have reached the 'normal retirement age', generally 65 but see page 147 for more about retirement age, your employer can retire you. In order for your dismissal on retirement to be fair, your employer must first have given you proper notice, at least six months, and have properly considered any request you made not to be retired and any appeal. This, though, is an area of law that may change in future, as a long-running court case waiting for a European hearing argues that any arbitrary retirement age breaks discrimination law.

Finally, if the employer can show that the reason for the dismissal was one of those listed above, the tribunal will consider whether or not the employer acted reasonably by dismissing you rather than taking some other course of action.

Shifting a shift?

Two security men, Ron Brown and John Pollard, were asked to change shift patterns as their employer thought this would lead to more efficient use of staff time. After consultation both refused but were sacked. Ron had been with the firm less than a year so could not make a claim but John was a long-service employee, and his wife was currently ill. He claimed unfair dismissal, but lost.

The tribunal agreed that their refusal to change their shift patterns did harm the business interests of their employer. John's dismissal was therefore a potentially fair dismissal under the category 'some other substantial reason'. This shows that in some circumstances you cannot rely on your contract of employment.

The tribunal will usually concentrate on whether the employee was 'reasonable' in resisting change, and whether the employer was 'reasonable' in insisting on the change. If the employer can show an overriding business need for the change then the tribunal will tend to decide in the employer's favour.

Qualifying conditions

If you think you have been unfairly dismissed, you may complain to an Employment Tribunal. In most circumstances, you must be an 'employee' (see Chapter 1) and have worked continuously for one year for the same employer. Members of the police force and armed forces cannot claim unfair dismissal.

The qualifying period of one year is not always necessary. It is reduced to one month where you are dismissed on medical grounds because of some health and safety requirements. There is no length of service requirement at all to make a complaint of unfair dismissal if you are sacked because:

■ You are pregnant, or for any reason connected with maternity.

■ You are a trade union member or because of trade union activity (or because you have refused to join a union).

■ You have taken some action to enforce your workplace rights – 'seeking to assert a statutory right' in legal jargon. A common cause is asking to receive a written statement of employment particulars after two months of employment.

■ You have refused to do something on health and safety grounds (see page 114 for details on what you can and cannot refuse to do).

■ You have 'blown the whistle' on malpractice in the workplace (see pages 27–28).

■ You have refused or are proposing to refuse to do shop work or work connected with betting on a Sunday (see page 23).

■ You are acting as a representative of employees for consultation on redundancy or a business transfer, or have put yourself forward as a candidate to do this. This might happen in a work-place where there is no recognized trade union as, in some circumstances, an employer must organize elections for work-force representatives so that they can consult with their staff.

■ You are an employee pension fund trustee or proposing to become one and have been sacked because of your role.

■ You have represented a fellow worker at a grievance or disciplinary hearing, or because you have asked to bring a fellow worker or a trade union representative with you to such a hearing.

■ You have campaigned for or against statutory trade union recognition.

■ You have taken part in lawful industrial action and have been dismissed for doing so within the first 12 weeks of that action.

You must make a complaint of unfair dismissal to a tribunal within three calendar months of the 'effective date of termination' of your employment (usually the date of leaving the job). Tribunals do have the power to consider claims made late if they consider that it was not 'reasonably practicable' to get the claim in on time, but in practice they are very reluctant to do this. It is always best to get an application in early, even if you subsequently withdraw it.

Tribunal procedures are explained in more detail in Chapter 8, which also sets out a number of alternative ways of settling a case, once you have made a claim, that do not involve the stress of a full hearing, and these are certainly worth considering.

If you do proceed to a hearing for unfair dismissal a tribunal will first establish that you were an employee and that you have been dismissed. It will then establish whether the statutory minimum disciplinary procedure was followed. If the employer has not followed the statutory procedure the dismissal will be automatically unfair. If the procedure has been followed correctly the tribunal will then consider whether the dismissal was fair or unfair. If it decides the dismissal was unfair it will then decide what to do about it.

There are three possible remedies a tribunal can order. These are reinstatement, re-engagement or compensation. Orders for reinstatement or re-engagement normally include an award of compensation for the loss of earnings in the period between the dismissal and the reinstatement (see Chapter 8 for more details). The difference between reinstatement and re-engagement is that reinstatement gives you your old job back, while re-engagement gives you a different, but comparable job.

As a result of age discrimination laws, you can now claim unfair dismissal even if you have reached the 'normal retiring age'. This is 65 unless a lower retirement age generally applies in your workplace. However, your employer can still retire you at the normal retirement age, and this will be a fair dismissal as long as your employer has properly notified you in advance of your retirement date and considered any request you make not to be retired. These provisions may change in the future because they are being challenged under EU laws on age discrimination.

There is no specified lower age limit for claiming, although it is illegal to work when you are under 13. Those defined by their employers as 'apprentices' cannot be dismissed unless their contract specifically says that they may be.

Non-UK companies

The law has recently changed, allowing you to claim if you are employed outside the UK if the employment relationship is closely connected with Great Britain, for example if the employer conducts their business in Great Britain, or if you are working in a British 'enclave' such as a military base.

There are special regulations relating to those employed offshore, that is, on ships or oil rigs. UK workers posted in EU countries are entitled to all the employment protection that applies to nationals of the particular country in which they are working. This area of the law is complex. If you are working abroad or working in the UK for a foreign-owned company you should take further advice from your union or one of the sources listed at the end of the book about making a claim for unfair dismissal.

Redundancy

Redundancy is sometimes used as a polite word for getting the sack, but it has a precise legal meaning and you have special rights if you are made redundant. In particular many have a right to redundancy pay. A redundancy is a dismissal caused by the employer's need to reduce their workforce. It may come about because a workplace is closing down, or because fewer employees of a particular kind are (or are expected to be) needed.

Normally, your job must disappear. It is not a redundancy if your employer immediately takes on someone else to do your job. This does not mean your employer cannot take on workers of a different type, or at some other location (unless the redundant employees could be required under their contracts to move to the new location). But it is still a redundancy if someone else already working for your employer moves into your old job as long as there is an overall loss of jobs. Providing some jobs end, your employer can shuffle existing staff between different jobs and functions.

Your employer must make a lump sum payment to you if you are made redundant, as long as you have at least two years' continuous service with them (excluding any service before the age of 18) and meet some other conditions.

In particular, you may not be redundant if your employer, an associated employer or another employer who takes over the business, offers you another job. But they must offer you a new job before your old contract expires and it must start within four weeks. However, the job must be suitable. You can turn down an alternative offer that is clearly unsuitable, or agree to try it out for a four-week trial period. You can agree with your employer to extend the four-week period in writing if you are being retrained. If at the end of the trial period you are still in the job, you will be deemed to have accepted it. This means that you lose any rights to claim redundancy.

If you reject the new job before the end of the trial period, because it turns out to be unsuitable as an alternative, or for good personal reasons, your redundancy will be considered to have started the day your old job ended. However, if your employer disagrees with your decision that the job is not suitable you may need to make a claim in a tribunal and show them why the job was not suitable. If it finds you have refused a suitable offer of alternative employment you lose your right to a redundancy payment.

Redundant?

Liz Acott was a lecturer at a college of further education. Her appointment was for one academic year, and was not renewed. This was not a surprise. There had always been doubt that there would be enough money in her department's budget to renew her contract at the end of the period of appointment. But when her appointment was not renewed Liz claimed for unfair dismissal.

The tribunal said that Liz's job was redundant, and redundancy can be a fair reason for dismissal. But they also held that the employer had a duty, as in any other redundancy situation, to try to assist Liz by considering her for other jobs they might have available. Since there was no evidence that the college had done this, she won her case.

What can you get?

The law provides a legal minimum for redundancy pay. Some employers will offer better terms, and some will include these in your contract of employment. The legal minimum depends on the length of your continuous service with your employer, how old you are and how much you are paid:

■ For each complete year of employment after your forty-first birthday you should get one and a half week's pay.
■ For each complete year of employment after your twenty-second birthday but before you turn 41 you should get one week's pay.
■ For each complete year of employment while you were either 18, 19, 20 or 21 you should get half a week's pay.

But, unless your employer or contract of employment is more generous, you cannot claim more than 20 years' worth of redundancy payments.

If you are made redundant you are entitled to a minimum period of notice. This is one week for every year you have worked for your employer up to a maximum of 12 weeks. If your employer makes, or lets, you leave before this minimum period of notice you should still be paid for the full notice period.

Working out how many years of service you have in order to calculate your redundancy payment is far from simple. The period starts with your first day with your current employer, and ends at what is called the 'relevant date'. This is the day on which your redundancy notice expires, even if your employer has let, or made, you stop work in the meantime.

It is calculated in calendar years, but with no fractions of a year. If you have worked for 10 years and 11 months, then it is counted as 10 years. The period must be of continuous employment. Days on strike do not count but do not break the continuity of the employment. Periods of maternity or parental leave do count and do not break the continuity of employment.

Other absences may sometimes count towards a period of continuous employment, even where the employment contract was broken, for example, by a temporary stoppage of work.

Calculating a week's pay

Working out your years of employment is only the first stage. You can then work out how many weeks' wages you should get. But not everyone is paid the same each week. There could be other arguments about which week to take and which part of your wages count.

The week's wage is taken to be what your contract of employment said you should have been paid in the week your employer gave you notice, for that week's work. If for some reason your employer did not give you formal notice, then it is the week in which they should have given you notice.

If your pay varies – for example, if you are paid on a piece-work basis – the amount is averaged over the 12 weeks immediately before the calculation date. Overtime and other bonuses only count if you are guaranteed them in your contract of employment.

But there is an upper limit of how much your weekly pay can be taken to be for the purposes of working out your redundancy pay. At the start of 2007 the limit was £310. It is uprated each year normally in line with the Retail Price Index.

Your employer may offset part of your company pension payment against your redundancy payment if you are dismissed not more than 90 weeks before the first pension payment is due.

You do not have to pay tax on a Statutory Redundancy Payment and it does not affect your right to claim unemployment benefit. You will not be entitled to Statutory Redundancy Pay if any of the following apply:

■ Your employment ends on or after your sixty-fifth birthday.
■ You work for a company with a normal retirement age of less than 65 and you have reached that age.

■ You are an apprentice whose service ends at the end of your apprenticeship contract.

■ You are on a fixed-term contract of more than two years' duration which includes, with your written agreement, a clause waiving your right to a redundancy payment, provided your employment ended at the appointed time.

■ You are a domestic servant working in a private household and you are a member of the employer's immediate family.

■ You are a share fisherman paid solely by a share of the catch.

■ You are a crown servant or employee in a public office or in the NHS covered by other redundancy arrangements.

■ You are an employee of the government of an overseas territory.

If your employer cannot pay because of serious financial problems, the Department for Business, Enterprise and Regulatory Reform (BERR) will pay you directly. They will only ever pay the statutory minimum amount even if your contract of employment promised you more. If your employer is insolvent, the payment is made by BERR and the debt is recovered from the assets of the business. If you have lost out because of a difference between the statutory minimum and what your contract offered you can make a claim against the remaining assets of the company, but a bankrupt company may not have sufficient assets to pay. In order to get payment from BERR, you must first have submitted a claim to the employer in the normal way, as described below.

Liability for making the payment rests with your employer. It should be made at, or soon after, the time of your dismissal. There is no need for you to make a claim, unless your employer fails to pay or disputes the entitlement. Where this happens, you should make a written request to your employer or refer the matter to an Employment Tribunal, or both, within six calendar months of the date your employment ended. If you do not claim within six months you may lose the right to a payment but the tribunal has discretion to extend this period by a further six months if you make a claim within those six months.

Consultation on redundancy

If your employer intends to make more than 20 people redundant over a 90-day period, they must, by law, consult the workforce. If your employer recognizes a union, it must be consulted. If not, your employer must establish a representative body, or make use of an existing representative body, for example, a staff council, elected by the entire workforce.

The agenda for consultation should include ways of avoiding redundancies or of reducing the numbers affected. Agreement does not have to be reached as a result of the consultation but the employer must consult 'in good faith', that is, with a view to reaching agreement. Certain information must be disclosed to the representative body including:

■ the reasons for the redundancies;
■ the numbers and descriptions of those affected;
■ the proposed method of selecting those to be made redundant – for example, 'first in, last out';
■ how any redundancy payments better than the legal minimum will be worked out.

Consultation cannot just take place one afternoon when the managing director has a spare half-hour. There are minimum periods during which representatives must be consulted. These are if 20 to 99 employees are to be dismissed at one establishment over a period of 90 days or less, consultation must last at least 30 days, and, if 100 or more employees are to be dismissed as above, consultation must last at least 90 days.

Individual notices of redundancy should not be issued until there has been sufficient consultation in line with these requirements. Any complaint that redundancy notices have been issued before consultation ends can be made to an Employment Tribunal. If the tribunal finds that a complaint is justified it can make a protective award, which will require the employer to pay the employees their normal pay for the period covered by the protective award. This is to allow for the consultation to take place before the redundancies are made.

Follow a path through the dismissal maze to find out your basic rights:

Are you an employee?

Not all workers are employees. As well as the obviously
self-employed, other workers can find that they are not employees in the strict legal
sense – see page 9.

Yes   No ▶

▼

Have you lost your job because:

you are pregnant;
of your sex, race, disability, age, religious belief or sexual orientation;
you refused to undertake dangerous or unsafe activities which posed a threat of
physical injury;
you tried to join a union;
you 'blew the whistle' on wrongdoing at work;
you asserted your right to be paid the minimum wage or took action against your
employer for a breach of employment law?

No   Yes ▶

▼

Have you worked for your employer for more than one year?

Yes   No ▶

▼

➤ There's probably nothing you can do, but it may be worth seeking further advice based on your own circumstances.

➤ You have probably been unfairly dismissed.

You can take a case to an Employment Tribunal. It does not matter how long you have worked for your current employer – all dismissals on these grounds are automatically unfair (though employers will normally say that dismissal was for another reason).

➤ There may be nothing you can do. Unless your dismissal came about through one of the special cases above, your employer can dismiss you without saying why. However, you should look at your contract of employment. If this contains procedures such as notice periods or the promise of a formal hearing that were not followed then you may very well have a case. Seek advice.

Does your employer say you are being made redundant?

No

Yes ▶

▼

Has your employer followed these procedures properly?

You may have a case. Take advice.

No

Yes ▶

▼

Have you lost your job because:

you cannot do it properly;
of serious misconduct by you;
of some legal requirement;
you are over 65 and made to retire.

No

Yes ▶

▼

If your employer cannot prove that you have been dismissed for one of these reasons then you have been unfairly dismissed.

➤ You are only redundant if your job has ended, and no one is being taken on to do your job.

Employers may select people for redundancy but they cannot discriminate on grounds of sex, race, disability, age, religious belief or sexual orientation.

If there are any procedures for redundancy in your contract of employment then these must be followed.

If there are more than 20 redundancies in a 90-day period then your employer must consult with the workforce. If there is a recognized union this must be with union representatives. If there is no union then special representatives must be elected. The consultation allows representatives to argue that the company should think again, to change the criteria by which people are selected for redundancy (say by increasing redundancy pay or early retirement pensions and asking for volunteers) and/or to argue for more help such as training or job search for those who are to go.

➤ You are entitled to redundancy pay if you have worked for your employer for more than two years. The amount depends on your age, length of service and pay. Many employers will be more generous than these legal minimums: aged 18–21 – half a week's pay for each year of service; aged 22–40 – one week's pay for each year of service; aged 41 or over – one and half week's pay for each year of service.

But weekly pay of more than £310 is not counted and no more than 20 years' service can be taken into account

➤ As long as your employer has followed proper procedures then you can be fairly dismissed for any of these reasons.

However, if you have any doubts you should take advice. You may have a successful tribunal case if an employer has not got a fair system for judging conduct or capability. Any employee facing a disciplinary hearing can take a workmate or union official in with them. If this is denied then you may have a case.

A tribunal may also disagree with an employer's judgement that your misconduct was serious enough to be punished by dismissal or that you could not do your job properly.

If you are over 65 then your employer can force you to retire, but this is being challenged and may change in the future.

8

Enforcing your rights

Employers may deny you your legal rights for a number of reasons. They may simply not understand the law or fully appreciate their responsibilities as employers. While this is no excuse, there have been considerable changes in employment law since the 1997 election and it is perhaps not surprising that some employers have simply not kept up to date, or fully understood some of the finer points of complex provisions such as the Working Time Regulations. Once someone points out their legal obligations, however, they are unlikely to continue to deny you your rights.

Other employers know that they are breaking the law but hope they can get away with it. If challenged they too are likely to back down. Sometimes anonymous letters have allowed workforces to challenge this type of employer without having to identify a 'ringleader'.

In other cases your employer may genuinely believe they are acting correctly and within the law, but you, and your advisers, may disagree. Some of these cases are because there is room for more than one point of view, such as whether your misconduct was serious enough to get you the sack. These cases are likely to end up in a tribunal, or be settled through one of the alternatives to a tribunal hearing described below. In other cases the law may not be clear, and a test case will be necessary to settle not just your case but that of many other people in your position.

One example of this process was the series of court cases taken by Britain's trade unions that established the rights of part-time workers to join company pension schemes. They established that companies that did not allow part-timers to join the pension scheme were breaking European sex discrimination law. This is because in most organizations the part-time workforce is mainly female, while full-time workers are more likely to be men.

The basic principle was relatively easy to establish, but how much compensation those who missed out on the chance to join good pension schemes should receive was less clear, as it depended on complicated legal arguments about how European law affected British law.

Because there is a lot of new employment law, and much of it began in Europe, there are likely to be further important test cases in the next few years. When the law uses words like 'reasonable' where there are value judgements involved, it usually takes one or more test cases to establish what the courts are likely to consider to be reasonable.

Test cases involving large companies are not likely to cause bad feeling. No one would be surprised if a company, faced with a potentially big bill to compensate part-time staff who had not been allowed to join a pension scheme, tried to minimize the costs. Most companies would not take it out on the staff concerned.

But it is a different matter when you are taking on a company that deliberately exploits and bullies its staff. If it has sacked you unfairly then you have nothing to lose in taking action against it. But if you want to enforce your rights while still an employee you need to understand that even when the law is on your side, a vindictive company can still do a great deal to make your life miserable, particularly if you are acting on your own.

You do need to think through your options very carefully if you are in this position, and as we stress in so many parts of this book, you should take further advice. While the law is likely to be on your side (as soon as you take action to enforce your rights, you gain special protection against unfair dismissal, even if you have only just started working for your employer) there may be better ways to proceed, such as signing up fellow employees into a trade union and asking them to act on your behalf collectively so the employer cannot identify and victimize anyone. Some breaches of employment law can be investigated by external agencies such as the Health and Safety Executive, and you may want to call them in.

But if you do decide, after taking advice, that you need to take legal action then there are a number of different courts and tribunals that can hear claims relating to employment rights. Each has an appeal route if you or your employer wish to appeal against a decision. In the case of work-related welfare benefits, such as Statutory Sick Pay, claims are dealt with by a separate system of tribunals (see Chapter 2).

Employment Tribunals and the courts

Bodies known as Employment Tribunals deal with most work-related legal action. Until 1998 these were known as Industrial Tribunals. Employment Tribunals operate in England, Wales and Scotland. In Northern Ireland the system is similar but the tribunals are called Fair Employment Tribunals and can also hear claims relating to discrimination on the basis of political opinion, which is illegal in Northern Ireland.

These tribunals are specialist employment 'courts'. A tribunal will be made up of three people. The Chair will be legally qualified, and there will be two lay members, one of whom has been chosen as an employee representative and the other as an employer representative. As a panel, all members must exercise impartiality but the lay members will be expected to bring their employment experience to bear when judging the facts of the case. However, in some cases, the tribunal Chair will sit alone, particularly when there are any preliminary legal arguments. The tribunals are serviced by regional offices, which process the claims and arrange for the hearings.

Tribunals were originally intended to provide a relatively cheap, speedy and informal means of settling employment rights disputes between employees and employers. While they are still less formal than civil courts, for many cases they have become more legalistic and formal as the law has become more complex.

However, most claims at tribunals are about unfair dismissal. Argument is therefore normally about the facts of the matter, rather than legal points, and you do not necessarily need legal representation – a union officer or advice worker may be better.

Civil courts

Not all employment-related cases go to a tribunal, and sometimes you can choose from a number of options. As we saw in Chapter 7, if you have been wrongfully dismissed – rather than unfairly dismissed – you can take a case either to a tribunal or pursue it through the civil courts. Civil courts, but not tribunals, can hear claims for breach of contract that do not involve dismissal, for example if your employer changes your contract without your agreement.

These courts can also hear claims for personal injury if you are injured in the workplace or suffer ill health as a result of your working environment and want to sue your employer for damages. For personal injury claims, you will need specialized legal help so we do not go into any detail here. Your union will probably have an arrangement with a firm of specialist lawyers and will pick up any legal costs. If you win, costs are likely to be awarded against the employer. If you are not in a union, then a local advice agency will be able to recommend solicitors who specialize in personal injury cases. Many solicitors will take such cases on a 'no win, no fee' basis if they think you have a good case. We would advise you to beware 'claims farms' companies that advertise in newspapers and on television. Some make inflated claims about what they can achieve.

A few employment-related matters might go to the criminal courts. For example, the Health and Safety Executive can prosecute employers who breach health and safety law. And if you do something illegal at work, such as stealing, or assaulting a colleague, you may be liable to criminal prosecution.

Where do I make my claim?

It is sometimes difficult to know *where* to pursue a claim. The rule of thumb is to check first to see whether the problem is covered by the list of issues dealt with by Employment Tribunals (see below).

You can make a claim at an Employment Tribunal under several 'heads'. For example, if your boss reduces your wages without your consent, and then sacks you without notice when you complain, on the grounds that you are black and he or she doesn't like black people, you can claim wrongful dismissal, race discrimination and unauthorized deduction from wages.

Some issues are not so easy to define. Common examples are stress and bullying at work (see Chapter 5). Sometimes these issues are directly related to another issue, which can be taken to a tribunal. Stress may be due to long hours, and working time issues can be taken to a tribunal. Bullying may include a sex discrimination aspect and this too can be taken to a tribunal.

Often it will not be so simple. You can, however, sometimes rely on the 'implied' duty in your contract of employment for your employer to provide a healthy and safe working environment (see Chapter 5). For example, if you are constantly being picked on by an aggressive line manager for no obvious reason, and your complaints to more senior management have been ignored, then you can try and sue in either a county court or the High Court, depending on the level of compensation you wish to claim.

Such cases are often complex and you are advised to seek help. A trade union will have expertise in assessing your problem and looking for redress in the right place. If you are not a union member then you could take independent legal advice, perhaps from a law centre. However, if you are not eligible for legal aid, then you may face considerable legal costs.

You cannot pursue the same claim in two courts simultaneously, even where they both have jurisdiction on such matters. The term court here includes Employment Tribunals. Neither can you bring a claim again in another court after you have lost it in the first one.

Claims can now be heard against employers who are based outside the UK as long as you are ordinarily resident in the UK. If you are a citizen of another EU country, posted in the UK, you can now claim protection under UK law and submit a claim to an Employment Tribunal or court. Similarly, if you are a UK national working in an EU country you are covered by its employment protection and can make a claim in its courts.

It may be that you do not want to go to court or to an Employment Tribunal, in which case you could try to negotiate a settlement of the matter with your employer. This is covered in more detail later on in this chapter.

Cases dealt with by Employment Tribunals

These are the main areas of employment law dealt with by tribunals:

■ equal pay;
■ sex discrimination;
■ race discrimination;
■ disability discrimination;
■ business transfers;
■ discrimination on the basis of age, religious belief or sexual orientation;
■ discrimination on the basis of trade union membership/non-membership, or activities;

- time off rights for pension fund trustees, trade union and safety representatives;
- wages issues, including national minimum wage and unlawful deductions;
- wrongful dismissal (breach of contract);
- unfair dismissal;
- redundancy;
- 'whistle-blowing';
- working time and part-time working;
- the right to be accompanied, or to accompany a colleague, at a disciplinary or grievance hearing in the workplace;
- the right to campaign for or against trade union recognition;
- dismissal for taking lawful industrial action;
- parental leave, maternity leave, paternity leave, adoptive leave, leave for family emergencies;
- dismissal for asserting a statutory right;
- written statement of employment particulars;
- written reasons for dismissal;
- failure to consider reasonably an employee's application to work flexibly.

Making a claim

Where your claim is about anything other than an actual dismissal, in most cases before you can bring a claim to an Employment Tribunal you must first have put in a written grievance to your employer. This is to encourage you and your employer to try to resolve things in the workplace without the need to go to a tribunal and has been made compulsory by the statutory dispute resolution procedures. If you are a union member you can seek help from your union representative with putting in your grievance.

It is not difficult to make a claim to an Employment Tribunal. The first step is to fill out a form called an ET1. These are readily and freely available. You can get one from a Jobcentre, ACAS, your union, a local advice agency or the regional or national Employment Tribunal offices (see the address section in Chapter 9). Although these forms are not difficult to fill in, it is very important to ensure that nothing that will help your case is left out and nothing that will damage your case is included.

Seek help from your trade union, or from a Citizens' Advice Bureau (CAB). While a CAB will give free assistance with filling out the form and general advice on your claim, it cannot represent you at the tribunal. Your union will normally provide representation if it judges that your claim is likely to succeed, though it may not take forward cases that it considers weak. This is not a judgement of whether or not you have been treated badly by your employer, but a judgement on whether you will succeed at the tribunal. These are two quite different issues. Once you have submitted the ET1 you will become known as the 'claimant'.

It is crucial that you stick to the time limits. For most cases, applications must be made within three calendar months of the 'effective date of termination' (usually the day on which you finish work) but there are some variations. See the timetable on pages 37–43 for all the time limits. It is very hard to persuade a tribunal to accept a claim that is 'out of time', even if only by a day. It is worth using recorded delivery so that you can prove when you posted the application, in case it arrives late because of postal difficulties beyond your control.

If your claim is one that is not about actual dismissal, so that the statutory disciplinary procedures don't apply, then it is likely the statutory dispute resolution procedures mean that you will have had to put in a grievance. If this applies then the normal time limit is extended by three months once you put in your grievance. However, you must allow your employer 28 days to respond to your grievance before you can put in your claim to the tribunal. If your claim is one where you have to put in a grievance and you don't put one in then the Employment Tribunal is unable to hear your claim.

There is no legal aid available for representation at Employment Tribunals, although basic preliminary advice can sometimes be obtained under the Legal Help scheme. This provides a short session with a solicitor to talk through any legal issue on a preliminary basis. Costs are not often awarded at tribunals, so you are unlikely to run the risk of having to pick up your employer's legal bill if you lose the case. In future the tribunal may decide to award costs based on the amount of time spent by you or your employer on preparing your cases. In addition, if you pay somebody to represent you at the tribunal and he or she wastes time and is incompetent, he or she may be liable to costs. This will not apply if he or she is representing you for nothing – for example, if you are represented by a trade union official or advice agency worker.

It is possible to represent yourself at a tribunal. The panel hearing the cases will try to help you. Although some people do successfully represent themselves, particularly in simpler cases, it is always best to try to have your own representative who is familiar with the way tribunals work. This is particularly important if your employer is going to be legally represented, and many automatically do this. You do not necessarily need to be legally represented. Union full-time officers are very experienced in taking cases to tribunals. If you are not in a union then you can consider employing your own solicitor, although as costs are not usually awarded at tribunals you will not normally be able to claim legal costs back from the other side if you win. Some advice agencies may be able to provide someone to represent you.

On the ET1 you will be asked to indicate the 'head' of claim. This means the category of jurisdiction into which the claim comes. This will be one from the list above, for example, unfair dismissal. You do not need to cite the legislation by its proper name, although if you can it does have the advantage of making the basis of your complaint absolutely clear to the tribunal.

You will also need to give details of the complaint and the remedy you are seeking. With any dismissal case you are advised to ask for reinstatement or re-engagement. You are highly unlikely to get it – on average less than 1 per cent of claims result in reinstatement or re-engagement – but it seems to have the effect of increasing the compensation, which you will probably get instead. It is also worth stating that you would like your claim to be heard by the full panel, as tribunals are increasingly trying to hear claims, at least at the preliminary stages, with the Chair sitting on his or her own. The advantage of the full panel is that there will be one member who has direct experience of your 'side' of the argument and you may get a more balanced judgement, at least on the facts.

You must be clear about whom the claim is against. If it is a discrimination or equal pay claim, the employer can be sent a questionnaire (see Chapter 7). After receiving the ET1, the tribunal can ask you to give a written answer to a question if it thinks that this would provide helpful clarification. It is important to do this if it should ask, as it may help your case.

The ET1 has to be sent to the Employment Tribunal's office nearest to the employer's business (the address is given on the form, and a helpful guidance booklet will be enclosed with the form). Your form and an ET2, which is a summons, are sent to the employer, who is known as the 'respondent'. Bear in mind that the employer will see everything you have written on your form, as will the tribunal panel, so be clear, be accurate and be polite! The employer then has to return an ET3 form, known as a 'notice of appearance', in which they will set out their defence.

Most employment rights are subject to eligibility requirements. The tribunal will first check that you are eligible to bring the case you have submitted. This includes checking whether you have first put in a written grievance if your claim is one of those where this is required. If you are not they will reject your claim. If there is any doubt then there will be a preliminary hearing, usually involving just the Chair.

For example, to claim unfair dismissal, you must be an 'employee' in legal terms and normally have worked continuously for your employer for a year or more and you must send the form in within three calendar months of the 'effective date of termination' (normally your last day at work). If you do not meet any of these conditions then the tribunal will reject your claim. Each chapter of this book explains the eligibility requirements in each case and on pages 37–43 there is a timetable showing the time limits for each type of claim. These are all subject to the three-month extension where you have complied within the initial time limit with the requirement to first put in a grievance. For unfair dismissal claims the time limit is extended by three months if at the end of the initial three-month period you are still waiting for the outcome of your appeal under the disciplinary procedure.

When the ET3 is sent to the employer, a copy is sent to ACAS, who will offer you and the employer conciliation to try to settle the claim out of court. You are under no obligation to accept conciliation but assistance from ACAS, which is free, can be very useful at this stage. For most claims there will be a fixed period of ACAS conciliation before your hearing can take place. There is more about alternatives to tribunal hearings in Chapter 7.

If the tribunal decides that your case has no reasonable chance of success, it can hold a pre-hearing review, at which it may require you to pay a deposit of up to £500, which you will lose if you lose the case.

How tribunals work

There is a complex set of rules governing tribunal procedures and tribunals have considerable discretion in how to handle cases. You should provide as much supporting written evidence in advance of your hearing as possible. This is known as 'disclosure' in tribunal jargon. The tribunal can order both you and the employer to provide more evidence if it wants. It normally expects to see items such as written warnings, statements from witnesses, copies of the company disciplinary procedure, and pay statements. Either you or the employer may ask the tribunal to order disclosure of documents before the hearing if you feel that they are necessary to make a fair decision. The tribunal can also make witness orders, requiring witnesses for you or the employer to attend.

The tribunal will normally meet within six months from when you first submitted your ET1. It will tell you and your employer when the hearing is due. You or the employer can apply for a postponement if there is a genuine difficulty with the required time. Most tribunal hearings are held in large rooms, rather than formal courtrooms. The three members of the panel will sit at the front, with the parties to the case and their representatives sitting opposite on the front row of chairs with others behind. Tribunal hearings are open to the public unless a specific request is made to the tribunal for a closed hearing and the tribunal agrees to this. This is normally only done in cases of great sensitivity – for example, involving sexual harassment, or where there are implications for national security.

Both parties can make an opening statement, presenting their case. Generally, the employer, or their representative, goes first but this depends on the nature of the case. An important consideration for the way the case proceeds is where the burden of proof lies. In some cases the onus is on you to show that your employer acted illegally. In others it is up to the employer to show they acted legally. For example, if you have been dismissed while you are pregnant, it is entirely up to the employer to show they had good reason to sack you. In other words, the tribunal will assume you were dismissed unfairly unless your employer can prove that they sacked you fairly. In other cases (such as constructive dismissal) the burden of proof is with you, and you therefore have to prove your employer was in the wrong.

After the opening statements the tribunal will then go on to hear each side's evidence, allow the other side to ask questions in cross-examination, examine the documentation, and finally call for closing statements from both parties. The tribunal can adjourn the hearing if time runs out or if either party wants to consider a settlement out of court at any time during the hearing. It can also stop proceedings if the respondent decides to concede the case, or if the tribunal decides that one party or the other is the clear winner and nothing would be gained by continuing the hearing. The panel will then decide whether you have won the case, and if so what compensation or other award you should receive. Each member of the three-person tribunal has an equal say, so it is possible for the lay members to outvote the Chair. However, panels generally try to reach a consensus. For straightforward cases, the decision will be given orally that day, with written confirmation and fuller reasons communicated in writing a few days later if requested. A tribunal can delay making a decision in a more complex case.

Awards at Employment Tribunals

The tribunal can order reinstatement or re-engagement but this is very rarely done in practice. Even when tribunals make such an order, employers commonly refuse to implement it. If your employer refuses to comply, you have to apply again to the tribunal. It will probably award you additional compensation in such a situation.

If your employer still refuses to comply, you have to pursue the matter in a county court (sheriff's court in Scotland). Ultimately, your employer cannot be forced to take you back and the final penalty is compensation. If this cannot be recovered, you have to pursue the matter in the county court. Unfortunately, the costs of doing this often outweigh the benefit, although if your union is supporting you, the cost will be to the union rather than you.

Most often the tribunal will order compensation to be paid. A table showing the upper limits for compensation for the various types of claim is given on pages 37–43. For discrimination claims, there is no upper limit and the compensation normally includes an element to cover hurt to feelings. For unfair dismissal the upper limit is £60,600. For wrongful dismissal claims in the tribunals, it is £25,000. These are upper limits, however, and usually compensation awarded is well below these levels.

Compensation for unfair dismissal includes an element to compensate for loss of earnings for the time between the dismissal and the tribunal decision. If you have got a new job, this element will be reduced to take account of what you are being paid. The compensation will also reflect other losses, such as loss of pension rights.

The tribunal will also order a 'basic' award based on your length of service. As with a redundancy payment, the amount you get will depend on your length of service, how old you are and how much you are paid:

■ For each complete year of employment after your forty-first birthday you should get one and a half week's pay.
■ For each complete year of employment after your twenty-second birthday but before you turn 41 you should get one week's pay.
■ For each complete year of employment below the age of 22 you should get half a week's pay.

There is an upper limit on the compensation for loss of earnings for the basic award, which is uprated annually in line with the Retail Price Index. It is currently set at £310 a week. In some circumstances, employers can be made to pay more compensation if they failed to let you use an internal disciplinary procedure. Similarly, your compensation may be reduced if you refused to use one. Your compensation can also be reduced if you are found to have contributed to your dismissal, or if your employer has already paid you some money, such as a redundancy payment for example.

Appeals

If you lose the case, you can request the tribunal to review its own decision. You must do this at the hearing or within 14 days of the decision being recorded. The grounds for doing this are limited, though. You would be likely to succeed, for example, if one of the parties was absent for part or all of the hearing, or if new evidence unexpectedly becomes available, but not simply because you thought the decision was wrong.

An appeal is also possible to the Employment Appeal Tribunal (EAT), which sits in London for England, Cardiff for Wales and Edinburgh for Scotland. The EAT is a special appeal tribunal that only deals with employment-related issues, nearly all on appeal from the Employment Tribunals. The appeal has to be lodged within 42 days of the tribunal decision. A special form is required, which can be obtained from the Employment Tribunal office or directly from the EAT (see address at the back of the book). Appeals are only allowed on a point of law but this can include a 'perverse' decision by the tribunal where, for example, the members did not understand the facts. You will need to ask the tribunal for a copy of the full written reasons for its decision and in some cases a copy of the Chair's notes, which you will also have to request from the tribunal. It is possible to get legal aid for representation at the EAT and, as it will essentially be dealing with points of law, it is important to be properly represented by your union or by a solicitor. Unions may have in-house solicitors who will represent you, or may engage a solicitor for you and pay the costs. Your employer can also appeal.

Leave

Jackie Kuti was granted extended leave to visit her family in Nigeria. Before she went she signed a document headed 'contractual letter for the provision of holiday entitlement'. This letter made clear that Jackie agreed to return to work on 28 September. It said: 'If you fail to do this your contract of employment will automatically terminate on that date.'

When Jackie returned to England on 26 September she fell ill, and was unable to go back to work on the 28th. Her employers considered that her employment had ended automatically according to the letter, and wrote to tell her so.

Jackie claimed unfair dismissal. She lost at both a tribunal and the Employment Appeal Tribunal. They ruled the letter was quite clear and that Jackie had breached her undertaking to return to work.

But the Court of Appeal disagreed. It ruled that Jackie had been asked to sign away her legal rights to be protected against unfair dismissal. But the law is clear that you cannot give up legal rights this way (with the exception of the right to redundancy payments if you are on a fixed term contract). Basically she had been asked to give up a right in return for an extended break.

This was an important test case. Following the judgement, employers cannot use 'automatic termination' clauses to get out of their duty to act reasonably in dismissal cases involving 'overstayers'. It is possible that similar 'automatic termination' clauses in other situations may also be found to be invalid on the same grounds.

Appeal from the EAT is to the Court of Appeal, but you need 'leave', or permission, from the EAT or Court of Appeal to do this. Appeal from the Court of Appeal is to the House of Lords. You will certainly need legal representation at these stages.

It is also possible for a tribunal or any of the courts involved at an appeal stage to refer a case to the European Court of Justice. Only cases involving important legal principles that derive from EU law will go to Europe. It is likely to be a slow and expensive process, in which you will need the support of your union, or an organization such as the Equality and Human Rights Commission.

It was not all right on the night

Jimmy Parker worked as a nightwatchman for his local council. He was sacked after being found absent from duty. He had signed the book as if he had worked a whole shift up to 7 am, but was found at home in bed.

Jimmy said he had gone home because he was ill, but he was dismissed on the grounds that he had absented himself from his security duties without permission and without informing his superiors or making an appropriate entry in the message/incident book. A general warning had been issued to all nightwatchmen a few weeks earlier to the effect that deliberate absence from duty would lead to dismissal. Jimmy had worked for the council for 27 years and had a previously good record of service. At a tribunal hearing Jimmy won a case of unfair dismissal on the grounds that given his age and record of service dismissal was an unduly harsh penalty. However, the Employment Appeal Tribunal reversed this decision. It said the council had acted reasonably because it had followed a fair procedure. Employees were aware of the consequences of such an action, and a proper appeals procedure had been exhausted.

As long as an employer follows a fair procedure it is up to the employer to decide whether or not to show leniency. It is not up to a tribunal to decide what it would have done in an employer's place. A clear message of cases like this is that as long as employers stick to a procedure that is more or less in line with the ACAS guidelines, then they are within their rights to dismiss you, as long as they apply the rules consistently, honour anything your contract of employment has to say about dismissal and do not discriminate.

Alternatives to tribunals and courts

There are various alternative ways of settling disputes with your employer that you should consider. Some of them will save you from having to pursue your claim in an Employment Tribunal or court.

You can reach a private agreement with your employer that they will pay you compensation, without necessarily admitting liability (indeed, employers normally insist on this). An employer will also often require you to sign an agreement, saying that you will drop the claim in return for the agreed compensation payment. You are best advised to negotiate such a deal with the help of a lawyer or a union.

A wiser option is to ask ACAS to conciliate a formal agreement between you and the employer, known as a COT3. ACAS does not charge for its conciliation services. By doing this, you agree to accept a stated sum of money as compensation for the dismissal. Once you have signed this you will be barred from pursuing that claim any further. ACAS has a great deal of experience in these kinds of cases, and can advise you on appropriate compensation amounts. This may be a particularly attractive option if you are not a union member and do not have the means to employ a solicitor to represent you at a hearing. A union may also advise you to go down this route.

A further option is to sign a 'compromise agreement', which is similar to a COT3 but need not involve ACAS. It must be signed by you and the employer and a person specified as having authority to sign compromise agreements according to the Employment Rights (Dispute Resolution) Act 1998. This will be a solicitor, a trade union officer or a CAB worker who has an appropriate certificate of indemnity insurance. Again, once you have signed a compromise agreement you cannot pursue that claim any further.

ACAS has recently established a new arbitration scheme for unfair dismissal claims. If you and your employer agree to go to arbitration, ACAS will appoint a qualified arbitrator, who will meet both of you in a formal hearing, probably, but not necessarily, in the workplace, hear both your arguments, listen to witnesses, look at relevant documents and then decide whether the dismissal was unfair. If the arbitrator decides that it was, he or she will order reinstatement, re-engagement or compensation exactly as tribunals do.

This new scheme has real advantages. It is informal and quick, it is easier to represent yourself, it will look primarily at the facts of the matter without having to refer to case law, and it is much more likely to award reinstatement or re-engagement than a tribunal. But there are also disadvantages. There is no right of appeal (although in exceptional circumstances judicial review may be available) and there are no lay members.

In general you should always take advice about which route is best for you in your particular circumstances. Your union or an advice agency, such as a Citizens' Advice Bureau, should be able to help.

Sources of advice and representation

You do not need to be a qualified lawyer to represent somebody at a tribunal. Indeed, it is wholly unnecessary to involve lawyers in many cases. Recently a number of independent advisers have started to advertise their services in local papers and by other means. They offer to prepare your case and represent you at a tribunal for a fee and/or a cut of your compensation.

You should be extremely wary of such advisers. While some may be competent, you have absolutely no guarantee that they have any expertise. The government is so concerned at just how badly some advisers serve their clients that they are currently considering whether they should be regulated. You should find out if their terms are reasonable. They may expect a very large share of any award you win. You should also discover their qualifications. Some claim that they have qualifications that they do not really have; others give themselves such names as 'legal advisers', which gives you the impression that they have some sort of legal qualification, when in reality this term means nothing.

The best representation you can have at an Employment Tribunal is probably a trained trade union representative. He or she will have considerable experience of how the tribunals work. He or she will also understand workplace issues and be able to spot errors made by your employer that an outside adviser would probably miss. Surveys have consistently shown that in cases where the applicant is represented by a trade union, the applicant is more likely to be successful and will get much better compensation.

If you are not a member of a union, you may be able to get free legal advice from a local law centre if there is one near you. Most larger towns and cities have them. Otherwise, ACAS can provide advice, though not representation, as can staff at a Citizens' Advice Bureau. If you do want to use a solicitor, make sure you choose one who has direct experience of Employment Tribunal representation as solicitors often specialize in particular areas of the law. Someone who sold your house may have no experience of employment law.

9

Further information

In much of this book we have stressed the need to take further advice about your own particular circumstances if you have a problem at work. This chapter shows you where to find it.

Useful helplines and advice services

workSMART from the TUC
workSMART is the TUC's online information resource, providing up-to-date information and advice on your rights at work. workSMART aims to become a one-stop shop for everything to do with working life.

The TUC website (www.tuc.org.uk) also contains employment rights advice and much up-to-date information about the world of work.

The TUC Know Your Rights Line
You can ring the TUC Know Your Rights Line on 0870 600 4 882. It can provide you with a series of up-to-date employment rights leaflets, which may add to the information provided in this book. It can also provide advice on an appropriate union for you to join. It is not staffed by trained advisers so cannot provide detailed advice.

ACAS public enquiry points

ACAS, the Advisory, Conciliation and Arbitration Service, is a publicly funded body that promotes good workplace relations. Its public enquiry point can provide advice on most of the rights at work issues covered in this book. It helps both employees and employers. Phone 08457 474747 (Monday to Friday, 8 am to 6 pm).

Or try the website www.acas.org.uk.

The Employment Tribunal Service

If you need information about making a claim or tribunal procedures you should call the Employment Tribunal Service Enquiry Line on 0845 959775 or go to www.ets.gov.uk.

The Department for Business, Enterprise and Regulatory Reform

BERR is responsible for many employee rights issues. The main website is www.berr.gov.uk.

To go straight to employment material, go to www.berr.gov.uk/employment, but the best official gateway to employment rights information is www.direct.gov.uk/en/ Employment/Employees.

The **National Minimum Wage helpline** number is 0845 6000 678. It is open from Monday to Friday, 8 am to 6 pm; all calls are charged at the local rate. All complaints about underpayment of the minimum wage will be treated in strictest confidence.

Alternatively, you can write to: National Minimum Wage, Room 91A, Longbenton, Newcastle upon Tyne NE98 1ZZ.

Further information about the NMW can be obtained from HMRC at www.hmrc.gov.uk/nmw.

Low pay units

Some parts of the country are covered by low pay units or similar bodies. These are voluntary organizations, not part of government.

Pay and Employment Rights Service (Yorkshire) Ltd
Tel: 01924 439381
www.pers.org.uk

Greater Manchester Pay and Employment Rights
Tel: 0161 839 3888
www.gmlpu.org.uk

Scottish Low Pay Unit
Tel: 0141 337 6819
www.slpu.org.uk

Discrimination advice
There is now a single official body that deals with equality and discrimination matters called the Equality and Human Rights Commission. It has a range of helplines.
www.equalityhumanrights.com/en/yourrights

Data protection
The Office of the Information Commissioner provides information and advice about the rights of individuals established under the Data Protection Act 1998 and the Freedom of Information Act 2000. Tel: 08456 306060 or 01625 545 745; www.dataprotection.gov.uk.

Whistle-blowing
Public Concern at Work can provide advice on 020 7404 6609; www.pcaw.co.uk.

Bullied at work
The Andrea Adams Trust
The Trust runs a confidential helpline on 01273 704900.
www.andreaadamstrust.org

Agency workers
The Department for Business, Enterprise and Regulatory Reform regulates employment agencies. It runs the

Employment Agency Standards Line on 0845 9555 105; www.berr.gov.uk/employment/employment-agencies. This helpline takes up complaints against agencies from agency workers on matters including non-payment of wages and dangerous working conditions. Complaints to this line can result in prosecution of errant agencies and even their closure.

The Recruitment and Employment Confederation (REC) on 020 7462 3260 or at www.rec.uk.com is the trade association for employment agencies. It sets standards for its members. If the agency you are employed by has an REC symbol on its premises or notepaper and you have a serious complaint about its behaviour, you can contact the REC who will investigate it on your behalf.

Health and safety
The Health and Safety Executive information line on 0845 345 0055 can help with health and safety and working time issues. It has a wide range of free leaflets, not just dealing with specific hazards but also providing help and advice for groups such as home workers or pregnant women. Most can also be viewed at www.hse.gov.uk.

Some issues are dealt with by the Environmental Health Department of your local council, including working time.

Working time
The Health and Safety Executive (see above) and the Environmental Health Department of your local council may be able to help and provide advice on your specific circumstances.

Family-friendly employment
Working Families has a helpline for people on low income who are lone parents or who have a child with a disability on 0800 013 0313; www.workingfamilies.org.uk.

The law and advice agencies
The Law Society is the national body for solicitors. It does not provide legal advice, but can give you details of local solicitors that specialize in areas such as family law or personal injury. Its number is 0870 606 2555; www.lawsociety.org.uk.

Law centres provide a free and independent professional legal service to people who live or work in their catchment areas. The Law Centres Federation will be able to tell you if you have a local law centre where you will be able to get free legal advice and possibly representation. Its website is www.lawcentres.org.uk.

You can also contact Community Legal Advice, which can provide free legal advice over the phone on 0845 345 4345. It also has a website, which includes employment law information, at www.cladirect.org.uk.

Citizens' Advice can tell you about your local CAB on 020 7833 2181, or try the website www.citizensadvice.org.uk. It also has web pages at www.adviceguide.org.uk with advice on your rights, including employment rights.

Your local library will also be able to advise you of other local advice agencies that may be able to help.

Tax credits and benefits
You can apply for tax credits online at www.hmrc.gov.uk/taxcredits and the website also provides extra information about tax credits. There is a special advice line to check your eligibility for tax credits or get a claim pack: 0845 300 3900, open 8 am to 8 pm, seven days a week.

Benefits national enquiry line 0800 882200. The local contact is your Jobcentre Plus office, www.jobcentreplus.gov.uk. There is a helpful overview and guide at www.direct.gov.uk/en/MoneyTaxAndBenefits/index.htm.

Criminal convictions
National Association for the Care and Resettlement of Offenders (NACRO) can provide help and advice for those with criminal convictions looking for work.
Tel: 020 840 6464; www.nacrodisclosures.org.uk.

Giving up smoking
QUIT 0800 002200; www.quit.org.uk.

Drugs
The National Drugs Helpline is on 0800 776600.

Alcohol
Drinkline is on 0800 917 82 82; www.downyourdrink.org.uk.

Britain's trade unions

If you want to join or contact a trade union, you can phone the TUC Know Your Rights Line, 0870 600 4882, or consult the worksMART website, www.worksmart.org.uk, which contains a union-finder to help you identify the most suitable union for you to join.

Jargon-buster

There is an even more comprehensive jargon-buster at www.worksmart.org.uk.

ACAS The Advisory, Conciliation and Arbitration Service is a publicly funded agency that provides advice to both employers and employees on industrial relations issues. It offers guidance, conciliation, mediation and arbitration upon request where there is a dispute between a worker, or a union, and an employer. It produces helpful Codes of Guidance on issues such as disciplinary procedures.

accident book A book that must be provided in every workplace by the employer, in which all workplace accidents must be recorded.

accredited training Training which is recognized by an official training organization.

additional adoption leave The second period of 26 weeks' leave that you can take in addition to 26 weeks' ordinary adoption leave.

additional maternity leave The second period of 26 weeks of maternity leave to which you are entitled on top of the 26 weeks of paid ordinary maternity leave.

advances of wages   Some or all of your wages paid before you have done the work.

agency worker   Someone who gets a job through an employment agency, which will 'place' him or her with the hiring company; the agency *or* the hiring company will be the legal employer, depending on the terms set out in the contract between the worker, the hiring company and the agency. Usually agency workers work under the direct control of the hiring company.

annualized hours contract   A contract that specifies the normal number of hours to be worked over the period of a year (rather than a day, or a week). This kind of arrangement can be used in sectors where there are seasonal fluctuations, such as making ice cream or Santa's grotto.

antenatal care   Appointments at clinics or hospitals for pregnant women, relating to their pregnancy (an appointment with the doctor for an issue that is not directly related to the pregnancy, such as a sprained ankle, would not count as antenatal care).

applicant   A worker who has submitted a claim to an Employment Tribunal or someone who has applied for a job.

apprentice   A specific legal term describing a person contractually bound to an employer to learn a trade or profession.

assert a statutory right   Ask an employer to give you something to which you are legally entitled; for example, a written statement of employment particulars or to be paid the minimum wage.

back pay   Wages or salary owed to you for work already performed.

bonuses　Extra money for good performance, high productivity, etc.

breach of contract　When either you or your employer breaks, or ignores the terms agreed in your contract of employment, either express or implied.

career break schemes　Periods of leave, paid or unpaid, offered by an employer for employees to pursue other activities; usually only allowed after you have been employed by that employer for a set period of time.

casual worker　A worker who is only employed when work is available, usually either on a temporary contract or on call when required to do a particular job or provide a service.

civil courts　Courts that deal with non-criminal issues, for example, matrimonial issues, commercial disputes and employment law.

collective agreement　An agreement between a trade union and an employer on behalf of a specified group of workers, usually relating to their pay and other working conditions.

comparator　A legal term used in equal pay cases – another worker doing a job comparable to your own.

compromise agreement　A legally binding agreement to accept compensation from an employer instead of pursuing a tribunal case; it must be signed by a solicitor, a designated trade union officer or a designated advice bureau worker.

constructive dismissal　If you leave a job because conditions have become so bad that you cannot continue you could claim constructive dismissal in an Employment Tribunal, or civil court. You argue that you were forced out of your job.

continuity of service   Having worked for the same employer for a continuous period of time, ignoring breaks for maternity, sickness, holidays and some other temporary interruptions.

contract worker   Someone employed on a short-term contract, usually to do a particular job. The contract will normally state when the employment will finish.

costs   When a court orders you to pay the legal costs incurred by the winning party, or when your costs are paid by the losing party.

COT3   A form used by ACAS when it conciliates an agreement between you and your employer that says you will accept compensation instead of making a claim at an Employment Tribunal.

crown servant   Some civil servants and government employees, who may have special terms and conditions of employment.

custom and practice   Something which has been done that way for a while. In particular, in employment law your contract of employment can change by custom and practice. For example, it may have become normal to allow staff to go home early on Christmas Eve and a court might decide that this has now been included in your contract of employment by custom and practice.

damages   Compensation when your employer causes you harm, either physical or in terms of your career prospects, injury to feelings, etc.

detriment   A legal term used to describe action taken by your employer against you unfairly, other than sacking you, such as refusing you training or promotion because you are in a trade union.

direct discrimination   A legal term meaning intentional discrimination, for example, saying that no women can apply for a driving job.

Directive   A piece of European Union law that applies in the UK.

disciplinary hearing   A formal hearing organized by your employer where you are required to attend and answer for unsatisfactory performance of some sort.

disclosure of documents   A legal term used when an Employment Tribunal requires you or your employer to produce particular papers for the hearing, for example, timesheets.

dismiss/dismissal   Legal term for sack, or termination of your employment.

duty of care   Employers owe you a duty of care. This means that they are responsible for ensuring that you are cared for at work and do not have to work in unsafe or unhealthy conditions. This can include protection against bullying or stress. An implied duty of care exists in all contracts of employment.

effective date of termination   The date on which you finish working for an employer when you are dismissed or your contract expires.

employee   In law someone employed under a 'contract of employment', giving him or her a number of statutory and contractual rights.

employment status   The legal definition of whether you are a 'worker' or an 'employee' or 'self-employed'.

Employment Tribunals Special courts of law which hear employment cases, for example, sex discrimination, unfair dismissal, non-payment of national minimum wage.

ET1 An application form on which you make a claim to an Employment Tribunal.

express terms Terms that are specified in a contract of employment, for example, the amount you are to be paid.

final written warning A final stage in a disciplinary procedure at work, after which you can be dismissed.

fixed term contract A contract of employment that expires on a date specified in the contract.

flexible working A broad concept that allows employees to adapt their working hours, times and even their place of work to suit their lifestyles and caring responsibilities. People with childcare or caring responsibilities who meet the eligibility criteria have the legal right to have their request for flexible working considered by their employers.

full-time There is no precise definition in UK law but generally considered to be working 35 hours a week or more.

further and better particulars A legal term meaning documentation to be used in a tribunal hearing, for example, references, records of disciplinary hearings.

gross salary or wages Wages before tax and National Insurance and other deductions, and including any other elements, eg performance-related pay.

guarantee payment The minimum amount payable to you by your employer if you are laid off, or told to go home until work becomes available.

implied terms   Terms that are not written into your contract of employment but are considered to be part of it, for example, a duty to provide a healthy and safe working environment for you.

incapacity   Usually, medical reasons why you cannot work.

indirect discrimination   A legal term for discrimination which was not intended as such, for example, a requirement that you had to work until 10 pm, which would indirectly discriminate against women, who are more likely to be the prime carers of children.

insolvency   When an employer is officially declared bankrupt.

itemized pay statement   A pay statement showing how your pay is made up. It will include terms such as basic pay, overtime, performance-related pay, gratuities and so on.

lay members   The non-legal 'side' members of an Employment Tribunal.

legal precedent   A ruling made in a court, which then influences future cases involving similar issues, often set by a 'test case'.

Maternity Allowance   Benefit paid to pregnant women/new mothers in some circumstances.

maternity certificate (MAT B1)   A certificate issued by your midwife confirming your pregnancy.

maternity leave   Time off work for pregnancy/childbirth.

national minimum wage   The least that you must be paid an hour.

notice of appearance   A document telling employers that they must respond to your application to have a claim heard by an Employment Tribunal.

notice of dismissal A letter, or sometimes a verbal statement, from your employer telling you that they intend to dismiss you on a certain date.

notice pay/payment in lieu of notice You may agree to accept payment of wages for your notice period instead of continuing to work until your date of dismissal.

notified day of return The date on which you tell your employer you will return after taking maternity or parental leave.

occupational pension A pension scheme provided by your employer (as opposed to the state pension or any private pension you have); you may or may not have to contribute to your occupational pension.

on call Available to work if required (typically social workers, security staff, etc).

ordinary adoption leave This is the first 26 weeks' leave to which you are entitled if you are adopting a child and have been continuously employed by the same employer for 26 weeks when you are told you have been matched with a child.

ordinary maternity leave The initial 26 weeks of maternity leave to which all employees are entitled.

out of time Missing the deadline for submitting a complaint to an Employment Tribunal.

overtime Hours worked over and above those specified in your contract.

parental leave Unpaid leave for all parents of children under five.

part-time There is no legal definition but generally anyone working fewer hours than full-time staff.

passive smoking Being exposed to other people's smoke.

paternity leave Two weeks' paid leave for fathers of either a newborn baby or an adopted child, who meet the eligibility criteria.

perverse decision A legal term meaning a decision which no normal or rational person would have made.

postponement Legal term used when a tribunal puts off concluding a hearing, or starting a hearing until a future date.

pre-hearing review Part of an Employment Tribunal procedure, when the Chair hears the basic details of a case and decides whether or not it is strong enough to proceed.

preliminary hearing Part of an Employment Tribunal procedure in which the tribunal will decide a preliminary qualifying issue, for example, whether or not you are an 'employee' in the legal sense and can proceed with your case.

protective award Where an Employment Tribunal makes a preliminary order to an employer not to do something such as making staff redundant, until it has had time to hear the case.

qualifying period A legal term meaning the length of time you have been working for your employer in order to qualify for certain rights, for example, you must have normally worked for one year at least before you can claim unfair dismissal.

reasonable adjustments Under the Disability Discrimination Act, an employer may be required to make certain adaptations to the working environment to allow a disabled worker to work for them, for example, installing a hearing loop facility.

recognize   The formal term for an agreement to negotiate certain workplace issues, for example, pay, or health and safety, with a trade union.

redundant/redundancy   When there is no longer the requirement for a job; the term 'redundant' specifically applies to the job and not to the individual doing it.

re-engagement   When an employee is allowed to go back to work after a dismissal to do the same or another job for that employer.

reference   Usually written, but can be verbal, report by a past employer, or from a school or college, or a responsible impartial adult, about the abilities of a job applicant to do the job for which they are applying, or a statement about how they did their previous job.

reinstatement   When you are restored to your previous job after a dismissal.

resigned   When you leave your job.

respondent   The employer against whom a claim is being made at an Employment Tribunal.

retired   No longer working, usually because of age but sometimes illness.

RSI   Repetitive Strain Injury; an injury or condition caused by doing the same thing over and over again at work, eg word processing.

self-certification form   When you take time off sick, for the first period you write a letter to your employer saying that you were off for whatever reason.

self-employed   Not contractually bound to an employer as 'an employee' though you may be contracted to provide a service to them; usually paying your tax and National Insurance yourself.

severance payment   This is not a precise legal term in the UK. Normally it refers to a payment made to you by an employer in return for you agreeing to leave without pursuing a claim against your employer.

sexual orientation   Your sexuality.

split shifts   Working part of a shift, then taking time off, then resuming work. An example might be working in a pub or restaurant for four hours over lunch-time and then working another four hours in the evening.

staff handbook   Explains how the company operates, its aims and objectives, and, usually, general terms and conditions of employment. It may be given to you when you start work and all or part is likely to be a legal document if it sets out some of your terms and conditions.

Statutory Adoption Pay   The minimum you must be paid during your adoption leave.

Statutory Maternity Pay   The minimum which you must be paid during 39 weeks of your maternity leave.

Statutory Paternity Pay   The minimum you must be paid during your two weeks of ordinary paternity leave.

Statutory Sick Pay   The minimum you must be paid when you are off sick.

suspension   When you are sent home from work, usually during a disciplinary procedure, often on full pay, pending a decision being made on whether or not to dismiss you.

temporary workers   Those engaged for a short time, or to do a particular job.

terms of your contract   What your contract says about your conditions of work; terms are legally binding on you and your employer once you have started working under them, and by doing so you have agreed to them.

transfers of undertakings   When a business changes owners, or an activity moves from the public to the private sector.

unauthorized deduction from wages   Money taken out of your wages without your permission and without it saying in your contract that it may be done.

unfair dismissal   Legal term for a dismissal carried out for no good reason or without going through an agreed company procedure for dismissals.

verbal warning   Usually part of a disciplinary procedure, a first warning, to be followed by a further warning, probably written, if you do not improve your performance or stop doing something wrong.

visual display units (VDUs)   Computer screens.

void   Legal term meaning a term in a contract that is not valid, for example, if your contract states that you will be paid less than the national minimum wage.

waive   A legal term meaning to agree to do without something.

whistle-blower   Someone who makes a complaint outside the organization for which he or she works about malpractice in the workplace. In some circumstances you are legally protected against detrimental action by your employer as a result.

witness orders   A legal term meaning an order in a court or tribunal to require a witness in a case to attend court or produce a statement.

worker   A legal term that goes wider than employee. The difference is that an employee either has, or is entitled to, a contract of employment. Someone who is a worker but not an employee works for someone else but usually on the basis of providing a service. Strictly speaking, all employees are workers, but not all workers are employees. In practice, however, worker is often used to describe those who are not employees.

written statement of employment particulars   A legal document, not strictly speaking a contract, in which your basic terms and conditions of employment are set out. However, your contract of employment may include your written statement.

written statement of reasons for dismissal   A legal term for a letter from your employer stating why you have been dismissed.

written warning   Usually the middle or final part of a disciplinary procedure, in which you are told that if you do not improve you will be disciplined or dismissed.

wrongful dismissal   A legal term meaning that your employment has been terminated in a way that does not follow the procedures in, or in some other way goes against, your contract of employment. A common example is not getting enough notice.

zero hours contract   A contract of employment which is legally binding on you, so that you are obliged to work when asked to, but which does not specify your hours and states that when you are not required to work you will not be paid.

Index

Index of advertisers